On Being the Church
in the World

BY THE SAME AUTHOR

*The Body : A Study in Pauline Theology*
*Jesus and His Coming*
*Twelve New Testament Studies*
*Honest to God*
part ed.: *The Honest to God Debate*
*Christian Morals Today*
*In the End, God . . .* ( James Clarke)

ESSAYS

# On Being the Church
# in the World

J. A. T. ROBINSON

*Bishop of Woolwich*

SCM PRESS LTD

BLOOMSBURY STREET LONDON

*First published 1960*
*Second impression 1961*
*Third impression 1964*
© *J. A. T. Robinson 1960*
*Printed in Great Britain by*
*Billing &˙ Sons Ltd*
**Guildford** *& London*

# Contents

# Preface

THE PIECES here collected were written, or in the first instance spoken, for very varied occasions, and I have not attempted to impose upon them any artificial uniformity, preferring to let their context and their date speak for themselves. They were written, with one early exception, at a time when my prime responsibility was the study and teaching of the New Testament. But they all represent 'applied' rather than 'pure' biblical theology.

The revival of biblical theology, which with the ecumenical and the liturgical movements forms the three-fold cord of renewal in the Church of our day, can, like either of the other two, become a diversion from the real involvement of the Church in the world. These essays are almost all concerned in some way with the relation between the Body of Christ and the body of this world, the body politic. But they are concerned with the theology of this relationship rather than with the practical and technical details, with the reappraisal that is demanded of the thinking, structure and preaching of the Church by taking history seriously both from the point of view of the Bible and of the world in which we live.

The conception of 'being the Church', as opposed simply to 'going to Church', is one that has brought new vision and vitality to many a congregation in recent years. But the rallying cry 'Let the Church be the Church!' can be perilous if it turns the Church in upon itself and allows it to forget that it exists always and only as the instrument of the *Kingdom*. The whole existence of the Church is orientated towards that area of life which, within this age, does *not yet* acknowledge the sovereignty of God established over it in Christ. The stress on the boundaries of this age, or *saeculum*, will explain also why in what follows it is impossible to be concerned with the witness of the Church in the 'secular' world without constantly becoming involved in the issues of eschatology.

Many of the things I have tried to say carry, I believe, far-reaching implications for the training of the Church's ministry; and I had originally intended to include in this collection two articles, 'The Theological College in a Changing World' and 'The Teaching of Theology for the Ministry', which appeared in *Theology* in June 1952 and December 1958 respectively. But these were thought to bear too specific relation to the English, and in particular to the Anglican, scene to be suitable for wider publication. I would refer to them, however, for some of the conclusions which I should wish to draw in this direction.

Part of the material has already appeared in print and this is republished with the kind permission of the editors of the journals concerned.

JOHN WOOLWICH

# CHAPTER ONE

# The Christian Society and this World: The Biblical Teaching[1]

SPEAKERS WHO START with a meticulous definition of their terms are always rather tiresome. It seems to cast a reflection either on their title (and by implication on those who gave it them), or on the mental finesse of their audience, or, more often, on their own ability to get on with the job. In my case, 'the Christian society and this world' would appear to be a good, plain, down-to-earth title. Everybody knows more or less what is meant by 'the Christian society'; and it would seem that anyone who is not quite out of this world knows what 'this world' is.

I have every sympathy with this common-sense point of view. Nevertheless, 'this world' is a phrase which requires closer scrutiny, and indeed will be the source of a great deal of trouble if it is not made clear from what precisely it is being distinguished.

It is a phrase which has entered our common speech through Christianity, though it is not peculiarly Christian in origin. 'This world' is not a combination of words that was used by classical writers, nor does it occur in the Old Testament. Moses or Isaiah would have been puzzled by it—for what world other than this might you be talking about? 'Heaven and earth' was a distinction they would have understood: but another *world* would have struck them as very odd.

By New Testament times, however, the phrase is quite at home. 'My kingdom is not of *this world*'; 'The form of *this world* is passing away': these seem to us natural and typical expressions— though the phrase is in fact used only by the two writers, St

[1] The first of the Stafford Cripps Memorial Lectures, delivered at St Paul's Cathedral, London, October 16, 1959.

John and St Paul, from whom those quotations are taken. But for its origins we must go behind Christianity, to the period between the Testaments. For in late Judaism two developments took place which were to lead men to differentiate between this world and another world. The first was the emergence of a belief in an after-life; the second was the distinction, drawn by the apocalyptists, between 'this age' and 'the age to come'. To examine our phrase in each of these contexts will help to clarify a number of points in the biblical teaching about the relation of the Christian society to this world.

I

The first contrast—between this present life and life after death —is the one which is normally implied by our own use of the phrase 'this world'—for instance, in the familiar prayer, 'Grant us in this world knowledge of thy truth, and in the world to come life everlasting', or in the words of the hymn, 'Free us from all ills in this world and the next'. 'This world' is the world this side of death.

As the particular concern of this lecture is with the teaching of the Bible, it is worth observing that this is not a biblical usage. The Bible never speaks of life after death as 'the next world', nor indeed as 'the world to come' (though the latter is, of course, a biblical phrase). Nor, I think, does its use of the expression 'this world' ever imply *this contrast*. It may appear to do so in such a passage as John 13.1: 'When Jesus knew that his hour had come to depart out of this world to the Father.' But for St John the contrast, here and elsewhere, is not between life before death and after it, but rather between the eternal being of the Godhead and the life of the *kosmos*, or the world alienated from God.

The nearest approach in substance to our modern usage, though it does not contain the actual phrase 'this world' is the verse in I Cor. 15.19, in which St Paul says, 'If in this *life* only we have hoped in Christ, we are of all men most to be pitied.' This is a very important text for the Christian's attitude to this world, and it is worth taking some trouble to try and understand what it means.

Everyone would agree that it says that if we are expecting all our cheques to be cashed in this life we are extremely foolish and deluded people. But where then, as Christians, *do* we expect them to be cashed? The obvious answer, it would seem, is in the life after death, in what we should call 'the next world'. But, simply on the grounds of biblical exegesis, I believe this answer needs to be questioned.

St Paul, you will remember, is at this point arguing with certain members of the Corinthian Church who said there was no resurrection (I Cor. 15.12). What was the precise issue between them? Was the Apostle claiming that the Christian hope had its centre in the life after death, and was it life after death that the Corinthians were denying? I think not. It is difficult indeed to be sure exactly what they were denying. But it is simplest, I believe, to suppose that the difficulty in Corinth was similar to the one that St Paul had encountered earlier in Thessalonica. The doubt of the Thessalonians was not whether there was life after death as such, but whether *Christians* who had died were going to be excluded from the coming Messianic reign. There was a general belief at the time, inherited from Judaism, that the dead would rise again at *the last day*, and, of course, these Christian brethren would be among them. But in the meantime they would have missed all they had been waiting for. The centre of the Christian hope was not life after death—most Christians of the first century did not expect to have to die in any case—but what St Paul calls 'the coming of our Lord Jesus Christ and our assembling to meet him' (II Thess. 2.1). And this was expected, at any rate according to popular belief, on earth. Hence the consternation when Christians began to die. They would not be there! Christ would come, and they would be in the place of the departed spirits awaiting the general resurrection. St Paul's answer was to insist that Christians, as men who had already passed beyond death with Christ, could not be excluded from his kingdom by the mere fact of their having 'fallen asleep'. Christ would 'bring with him' those who had passed from this scene, and those still here at the time would enjoy no advantage over them (I Thess. 4.14f.).

But, says the objector in Corinthians, 'How are the dead

raised? With what kind of body do they *come?*' (I Cor. 15.35). The very direction of the verb shows how different is the mental picture from that which we share when we speak of *going* to heaven. For the Corinthians, as for the Thessalonians, the living will already be here, in their bodies. But what of the dead, who will be 'naked' (cf. II Cor. 5.3)? St Paul's answer this time is to criticize very radically the whole popular expectation that the Messianic age will simply be an extension of this terrestrial order: 'Flesh and blood cannot inherit the kingdom of God, nor does the perishable inherit the imperishable' (I Cor. 15.50). The mere fact that on 'the day' a man may still have a body of flesh and bones will stand him in no stead. 'We shall not all sleep, but we shall *all* be changed' (I Cor. 15.51). And the transformation will be so radical that living and dead alike will be in exactly the same position. Hence death has lost its power to make any difference: 'O death, where is thy sting?' (I Cor. 15.55).

Now clearly it is not possible for us to accept this scheme literally. Indeed, St Paul's own words condemn the literalism with which it was taken in his day and has at times been taken ever since. It is the language of myth. But it is important to understand the framework of the myth with which the biblical writers were working if we are not to misinterpret their teaching. What St Paul is contrasting with hope 'in this life only' is not hope for life beyond the grave. (Most first-century Christians, as I said, including probably St Paul himself at that time, did not expect to have to die.) The contrast with what he calls elsewhere 'the life I now live in the flesh' (Gal. 2.20; cf. Phil. 1.22), the order of 'flesh and blood', is rather the Messianic reign or the kingdom of God.

This has an important corollary for our thinking today. It is often said that Christians can afford not to care over much what happens to this world, even if the whole thing is blown to bits, because their hope is set on the next world, their cheques, as it were, are cashable on 'the other side'. And the decline in our generation of any lively hope in the after-life is naturally viewed by this way of thinking as undercutting the whole Christian valuation. The Christian life without the life after death would be like discovering that the bank had no assets after all: the whole enterprise would turn out to be worthless.

Now no one wishes to deny that life beyond the grave is an essential part and presupposition of the New Testament message. It is a presupposition, in that it is not distinctively Christian. Jesus argued for it by pointing to the Patriarchs: 'God is not the God of the dead but of the living' (Mark 12.26f.). It is not, as so many Easter sermons maintain, something which is proved by the resurrection of Christ. St Paul's thesis is not, 'If Christ has not been raised, there is no resurrection of the dead', but rather, 'If there is no resurrection of the dead, then Christ has not been raised' (I Cor. 15.13).[1] The raising of the dead is his presupposition, and it is an indispensable part of the Christian preaching.

What is quite different is to say that it is the centre of the biblical hope. For much the greater part of the biblical period that distinctively Hebraic virtue, hope, was nourished and maintained without any living faith in an after-life. Again, contrary to what is usually supposed, the doctrine of the immortality of the soul, properly speaking, finds no place in the Old Testament or the New.[2] Moreover, as we have just said, the early Christian writers centred their hopes, not in life after death, but in the new resurrection order of 'life in Christ', which they entered at Baptism *and to which death could make no difference.*

Our generation, so far from being furthest removed from the outlook of the New Testament, is perhaps in this respect closest to it. The other-worldliness which, from the second century to the nineteenth, placed 'the new world' on the other side of the grave no longer exercises the same pull upon us. We are unable, like our forefathers, to rest everything on immortality or to define the purpose of life as 'making a good death'. Secularism has done its work in detaching us from that idol. Indeed the Marxist, with no belief in an after-life, is in a real sense closer to the biblical outlook than the Christian who pins everything upon it.

[1] See further my article 'Resurrection in the New Testament' in the *Interpreter's Dictionary of the Bible.*

[2] There are indeed traces of it in the Apocrypha, in the book of Wisdom, where Greek influence is discernible.

The Communist conception of 'the new world', as something that is coming *despite* the death of the individual, is at this point nearer to the New Testament, though in treating every generation but the last, and consequently every individual within a generation, as a means to an end, Marxism has a radically sub-Christian doctrine of man.

2

It is time, however, now to turn to the second distinction which arose in the inter-testamental period and which allowed the New Testament writers to speak of 'this world' in a way that the men of the Old Testament would have found quite unnatural. The first distinction was that between this life and the next life, though I have tried to show that it is no accident that the Bible never speaks of this as a distinction between two *worlds*. There is one world, God's world. The only difference is whether the individual is 'in the flesh' or out of it; and since 'flesh and blood' cannot in any case inherit the kingdom of God, it is a distinction without ultimate significance. That is the reason why it makes such surprisingly little difference to the Christian hope whether, as in the New Testament, few Christians expected to die before the End or, as today, almost all Christians expect to do so.

But the second distinction is of much more fundamental significance. This is the distinction between 'this age' and 'the age to come', between the world as it now is and the world as it will be in the consummation of God's purpose.

Again, it must be observed that the usual way in which the New Testament describes this distinction is not in terms of two 'worlds', but of two 'ages'. Both *kosmos*, world, and *aion*, age, are indeed used to describe it. The difference between them is obscured for the English reader by the fact that the Authorized Version regularly renders them both by the term 'world', though the Revised Standard Version very properly differentiates, as did the Vulgate before it with its distinction between *saeculum* and *mundus*. The word *kosmos* represents the Hellenistic way of putting it, while *aion* corresponds more strictly to the Hebrew *'olam*. But—and this is the important point—whichever term is used, the underlying presupposition is the *temporal* distinction made by the Hebrews rather than the spatial distinction drawn by the Greeks. Even when the New Testament writers speak of 'this world', they are differentiating life as it *now* is from life in 'the *age* to come'. The contrast is between 'the sufferings of this present time' and 'the glory that is to be revealed' (Rom. 8.18); it is not between terrestrial existence, which is due for the scrap-heap, and 'another country', 'above the bright blue sky', which is 'eternal in the heavens'.

To put it another way, the distinction between the 'other world' and 'this world' is not, as in our usage, the same as that between 'heaven' and 'earth'. For the Bible, earth is not to be scrapped in favour of heaven, or left behind in order to 'go to heaven'. The biblical promise is rather of 'a new heaven *and* a new earth' (Isa. 66.22; Rev. 21.1). And the word which it uses for 'new', *kainos* rather than *neos*, implies the *renewal* or restoration of all things, rather than a fresh start, as it were, on another site. Everything that has been done here, in the body of this existence, will not be lost, but be taken up and transfigured. And it is for this reason that St Paul concludes his great chapter on the resurrection with the call to 'be steadfast, immovable, always abounding in the work of the Lord, *knowing that in the Lord your labour is not in vain*' (I Cor. 15.58). There is an essential connection between this world and the next: they are the same divine creation, though the 'body' of it all is to be transformed out of recognition (I Cor. 15.43f.).

And it is as a corollary and not as a contradiction of this that he insists earlier in the same Epistle that 'the form (the *schema*) of this world is passing away' (I Cor. 7.31). What does he mean by such a phrase, and what does the New Testament as a whole mean by language like this, of which there is a good deal? Again, perhaps the best analogy for understanding it is provided by Marxism.[1] The Marxist has a strong sense that the system which

---

[1] These parallels are not fortuitous, for nowhere is the Jewish background of Karl Marx more evident than in his eschatology. See further my essay, 'The Christian Hope', in *Christian Faith and Communist Faith* (ed. D. M. Mackinnon), pp. 209-26.

determines the configuration of this present order is passing away. By that he does not in the least mean that history is coming to an end: on the contrary, history properly speaking, as opposed to pre-history, is just about to begin. History will go on, but it will no longer be determined by the dialectic of the class-struggle. In Pauline terms, it will no longer be subject to the *stoicheia*, the elemental forces, of this *kosmos*. The *kosmos*, in such contexts, is not to be understood to mean the world *per se*, the sum total of creation, but rather the order (a very literal translation of *kosmos*) whose pattern at present imposes itself on creation. It is this system or *schema* which is in the process of dissolution, and the purpose is precisely that 'creation itself' may be 'set free from its bondage to decay' (Rom. 8.21). When therefore the Christian society is told to repudiate 'the world', it is important to be clear what is meant. It is no more a call to 'other-worldliness', as that is commonly understood, than when the Communist party is ordered to refuse co-operation of any kind with the capitalist system. The Christian is not to be judged by his efforts at ameliorating 'the world' in this sense, any more than Communist activity is to be assessed by the improvements it effects in the capitalist order. On the contrary, 'the world' is to be repudiated: it is passing away (I John 2.17), it lies wholly within the power of the evil one (I John 5.19). It is the new world of Christ's revolution that alone claims the Christian's loyalty.

In such a context these familiar statements of the New Testament are intelligible. But once we understand 'the world' to mean what common sense means by 'this world' the effect is calamitous. The result is that Christians contract out of history altogether. Instead of being committed, like the Marxists, to a radical transformation of history, they become escapists from history. And Jesus' words to Pilate, that 'my kingship does not have its origin in this world-order', are interpreted to mean 'my kingdom has nothing to do with this world'.

### 3

I hope perhaps that what I have said so far has demonstrated the need for being careful about our terms. The only other-worldliness which the Bible encourages is the sort of other-worldliness, if that is the right term, of the Communist, who, like the Christian, refuses to let his thinking or his actions be conformed to the pattern of the present world-order (cf. Rom. 12.2). It is in this sense that the Christian is told, 'Do not love the world' (I John 2.15); and the dangerous ambiguity of the phrase is illustrated by the fact that this very same writer says that 'God so loved the world' (John 3.16) that for its life he gave his only Son.

That apparently contradictory combination is, however, no accident. It is bound up with the essential and peculiar paradox of Christianity. There are many other religions which say, 'Do not love the world': there is no other which says at the same time, 'God so loved the world that he gave', and whose central affirmation is of the Word made flesh. And it is this paradox which governs the distinctive style of the life of the Christian society in this world, which we must now go on to try and define.

For such a definition there is still no better place from which to begin than the famous passage in the anonymous Epistle to Diognetus, penned perhaps within fifty years of the New Testament period. Let me recall some sentences from it:

> Christians are not distinguished from the rest of mankind either in locality or in speech or in customs. For they dwell not somewhere in cities of their own, neither do they use some different language, nor practise an extraordinary kind of life ... But while they dwell in cities of Greeks and barbarians as the lot of each is cast, and follow the native customs in dress and food and the other arrangements of life, yet the constitution of their own citizenship, which they set forth, is marvellous, and confessedly contradicts expectation. They dwell in their own countries, but only as sojourners; they bear their share in all things as citizens, and they endure all hardships as strangers. Every foreign country is a fatherland to them and every fatherland is foreign ... Their existence is on earth, but their citizenship is in heaven. They obey the established laws, and they surpass the laws in their own lives ... In a word, what the soul is in a body, this the Christians are in the world ... The soul is enclosed in the body, and yet itself holdeth the body together; so Christians are kept in the world

as in a prison-house, and yet they themselves hold the world together . . . So great is the office for which God hath appointed them, and which it is not lawful for them to decline.[1]

Such a style of life is certainly not other-worldliness in the usual sense of that word: 'they bear their share in all things as citizens'. In fact, it is marked by the awareness of living, and living to the full, in two worlds at once. Yet it is equally far from what is meant by having the best of both worlds. The phrase which perhaps describes it better than any other is one coined by Dr Alec Vidler. He has defined the characteristically Christian way of life as 'holy worldliness'.[2] Let me try to draw out what I take that to mean.

First, the Christian style of life is marked by an extraordinary combination of detachment and concern. The Christian will care less for the world and at the same time care more for it than the man who is not a Christian. He will not lose his heart to it, but he may well lose his life for it. This, paradoxical as it sounds, is not, I believe, difficult to recognize for the authentic Christian attitude when we see it. The trouble is that we so seldom do see it. The Christian community is neither sufficiently detached nor sufficiently concerned. The Church's perennial failing is to be so identified with the world that it cannot speak to it and to be so remote from it that, again, it cannot speak to it. These would appear to be opposite and mercifully incompatible sins; but it is remarkable how easy it is for the Christian society and for the Christian individual to commit both of them at once.

Holy worldliness involves constantly walking on a knife-edge:[3] it is only too simple to slide off into becoming too worldly or too other-worldly—and neither is holy, though the latter has often been hailed as sanctity. To be concerned but not involved is just as great a temptation for the Church as to be involved but not concerned.

A second mark of the Christian style of life is an equally paradoxical commitment to what Dr Vidler has elsewhere called

[1] Epistle to Diognetus, 5 and 6. Trans. J. B. Lightfoot, *The Apostolic Fathers*, pp. 503-5.

[2] The title of a lecture reprinted in his *Essays in Liberality*, pp. 95-112.

[3] Cf. the striking chapter on Christian prayer written from this point of view in G. F. Macleod's *Only One Way Left*, pp. 146-63.

'evangelization' and 'civilization' at the same time.[1] There has been a perennial tension within the Christian tradition between saving men's souls and ministering to their bodies, between offering them the pure milk of the Gospel and proffering the cup of cold water. There are Christians who quite sincerely believe that the Church has more important things to do than to become involved in the latter concern, a concern which may lead very rapidly these days into the provision of water-mains and sewerage, hydro-electric schemes and Aswan dams, and so into the time-consuming, divisive and dirty business of politics. No, the Christian must give himself to spreading the Gospel and not allow himself to be diverted into filling bellies or filling forms.

But the dilemma is a false one, and comes once again from an unbiblical attitude. For preaching the Gospel in the categories in which Jesus himself preached it is preaching the gospel of *the Kingdom*, of the sovereign rule of God over the whole range of human life. And it is this kingdom, or commonwealth, of which Christians are the citizens and ambassadors within 'this world'. There is no department of the world's life into which they are not commissioned to go. They find themselves concerned with evangelization *and* with civilization, because in the long run (though not always in the short run) the two are the same—the bringing to men and society of the *civitas dei*, that divine commonwealth which must ultimately transform the kingdoms of this world till they become the kingdom of God and of his Christ. And the Christian style of life is the expression of the *total* design of God for his world, and not of one side of it alone or of the other. 'Only let your manner of life', says St Paul in Phil. 1.27, 'be worthy of the gospel of Christ'; and for 'manner of life' it is significant that he uses the same word, *politeuesthe*, which later in the Epistle he is to use of the Christians' *politeia*, or citizenship, in heaven; and which we use for 'politics'. Being worthy of the Gospel, evangelization, *includes* the concern for civilization. No definition of 'the spiritual life', of the individual or the community, which leaves out political engagement in the broadest sense of that term can claim to be true to the whole counsel of God.

[1] *Christian Belief and This World*, pp. 44-6.

4

This leads me, finally, to some closing observations on the *place* of the Christian society in 'this world'. I have just indicated that the Christian society, the Church, is the instrument of *the Kingdom*. And it is vital to keep this relationship clear. For the perennial temptation of the Church is to equate itself with the kingdom of God on earth, and so to regard itself as the only agent of God in this world.

Properly defined,[1] the Church is the society in which the universal kingship of God in Christ is *acknowledged*. It is the society, therefore, in which that kingship is embodied, or should be embodied, more fully than in any other section of humanity: it exists, in St James' words (Jas. 1.18), as 'a kind of first fruits' of God's redemptive purpose; it is the instrument by which the rest of creation is to be restored and conformed to the image of his Son.

But it is easy from this high doctrine of the Church to go on to regard it also as the instrument of God's *creative* purpose, to assume that what God is doing in this world he must be doing through the Church, that the space to watch, as it were, if one really wants to see what God is up to, is the Church papers. Now no non-Christian, it is safe to say, would ever imagine this. Nor—which is more important—would anyone reach this conclusion from reading the Bible.

In the Old Testament, the people of God is certainly not the rudder by which the course of history is steered. It is much more like a cork bobbing on the ocean borne this way and that, at times almost submerged, by the swirl and current of events. True, the biblical writers insist that it provides the clue to the *understanding*, and even more to the *redemption*, of this process. It is 'the saints of the Most High' rather than the secular world-empires which provide the pattern and the pledge of God's victory. But the answer to the question 'What is God doing?' is at any moment just as likely to be given in the operations of

[1] For a fuller statement of the relation between the Church and the kingdom of God, see O. Cullmann, 'The Kingship of Christ and the Church in the New Testament,' *The Early Church*, pp. 101-37.

Pharaoh, or the King of Assyria, or Cyrus King of Persia, as in any activity which today would be regarded as the work of the Church.

And in the New Testament, this is still true. It is most obviously true in the Book of the Revelation, the only New Testament book to deal specifically with the theology of the secular world. In it, though God is indeed acting *for* the Church, he is never contemplated as bringing about the consummation of history *through* the Church. What *is* to be done 'through the Church' is, as St Paul says in Ephesians, for the plan of God's redemptive mystery to be made known to the principalities and powers of this world (Eph. 3.9f.). The Church alone holds the clue to God's purpose; and holding that clue it has to be in the world, to 'redeem the time' (Eph. 5.16). It is the instrument of God's *reconciling* work (Col. 1.18-20). But though *creation*, the continuous creation of God's advancing purpose, is firmly declared in the New Testament to be 'in Christ' (John 1.3f.; Col. 1.15-17), it is never thought of as set forward specifically or primarily through the Church.

Obviously it is possible to press this distinction too far, for there is no final distinction in God between creation and redemption. But it is equally perilous to ignore it. The Church's task is to be wherever God is at work, in the van of his process, baptizing and transforming it in Christ. But, contrary to what is sometimes assumed, the Church cannot claim advance knowledge of God's plan of campaign, except in so far as it is given to the Christian prophet to see deeper and further into the mind of God *as he is actually about* his creative purpose. The Church can never say in advance what instrument, what channel, God will use or refuse. And any schema which implies that it can, that it has an inside knowledge of the pattern of history, is an idol. And this is true even, or especially, when that schema centres in the missionary work of the Church, as though this were the clue to the dialectic of events. The missionary work of the Church bears, indeed, a vital relation to the End (cf. Matt. 24.14): it is that through which the old is to be made *new*. But it is nowhere claimed in the Bible as the mainspring of God's action in history. The Christian society must always be expecting God to be acting decisively outside its ranks.

The purpose of these seemingly rather negative remarks is to urge that Christians be found in the right place in 'this world'. Let me end by putting the matter in terms of a parable. Last Good Friday two processions met, or rather were diverted from meeting, in the streets of Reading. The one was that of the Campaign for Nuclear Disarmament, on its march of protest from Aldermaston to London. The other was a Good Friday procession of witness by the local Christian Churches. What was the relation between these two processions in the purpose of God, and where should Christians have been? Clearly, they had a responsibility to the second, bearing their distinctive witness to the redemptive act of God in Christ. But may it not have been equally, if not more important, that some at least should have been in the first—as, of course, they were? If the concern for which that secular pilgrimage stood represents in any way a word of God to our generation, then the Christian's place is to be at the point which God has reached in his creative purpose, to be there to inform it with the mind of Christ, to redeem it from the 'powers of this present age'—and, last but not least, himself to be addressed and humbled by God through it.

The power to do all this will be given to him only through his membership of the Christian society. It is this alone (unless it lose its own savour) which, as the salt of the earth, will prevent 'this world' from going bad. It is the leaven of the new creation. But the leaven must always be in the lump. Christians may often be tempted to think how much purer it would be if it were kept out of it. For their involvement in 'this world', to be the soul in what St Paul has no hesitation in describing as 'this body of death' (Rom. 7.24), is always a call to share, not only in the sovereignty, but in the suffering and the endurance, which are ours in Jesus (Rev. 1.9). 'Christians are kept in the world as in a prison-house'. 'Yet they themselves hold the world together . . . So great is the office for which God hath appointed them, and which it is not lawful for them to decline'.

The committal to that warfare in which there is no discharge no one of our generation understood better than the great example of holy worldliness in whose memory these lectures stand.

# CHAPTER TWO

# The Social Content of Salvation[1]

THE CHRISTIAN GOSPEL is that salvation has been brought down from heaven to earth, that it is possible for the eternal life of God to become incarnate in the historically conditioned lives of men and women on earth. This means that, while the soul of salvation is eternally the same, its body is always changing. The particular ideal of life which in any age translates into a pattern of concrete social relationships the fulfilment of the human spirit in God requires to be redefined with every fundamental change in the structure of society. Salvation becomes disembodied, and therefore irrelevant (for it is through the body alone that men perceive the soul), when this redefinition is not made. And the fact that it has not yet been fully made in our generation lies at the root of the ineffectiveness of much present-day evangelism. What, in terms of his contemporary society, has a man to be delivered from and enabled to become, if salvation is to appear to him a relevant offer? Unless religious salvation at least includes social salvation, it is a thing without body and without power. Religion may offer a man a place and purpose in the ultimate scheme of things, but he is not likely to be remotely interested in it, unless he can see it as giving him in the first instance a place and purpose in the immediate setting in which he lives. It is when he sees the Gospel discovering to him social salvation, that is, a position in society in which he really finds himself, where he counts, is of value, and can make a difference, that a man may begin to understand a gospel promising him 'right standing' with God. The content of social salvation—what a man has to become

---

[1] Written in 1946, in terms of the British scene. Reprinted from *The Frontier*, November 1952.

in order to find fulfilment as a member of society—differs from society to society. Christianity must take account of these changes, as in the past it has done, if it is to continue to offer salvation from and to the things that are really relevant.

For the purposes of defining the content of social salvation, one can divide the types or stages of society into three main classes.

### 1. *Pre-scientific society*

Economically the basic fact here is man's *dependence* on nature for his livelihood. The key idea, therefore, for the understanding of its character is that of dependence. Society is hierarchical in structure, one class depending on another and in its turn having others dependent on it, in a system of graded privilege and responsibility. It is typified in Hindu caste-society and Western feudalism, and its structure still survives in the armed forces, where, like the centurion of old, the officer is a man under authority, having soldiers under him. Becoming a significant member of this society, acquiring value and the power to count in it, meant finding a place of dependence, however mean, in the social organism. The outcaste, the serf, the slave had no status in it. They possessed no rights; they were *aprosopoi*, without personality. They never became what it meant to be fully human in such a setting. For social salvation lay in aquiring some function as a member, or limb, of the body politic, on which in turn the health of the whole depended.

When the Church proffered salvation to this society, it held out to men what made possible also their ideal of social salvation. What it bestowed, of course, was not outward caste: it did not make every villein into a bailiff, every slave into a freeman. But it gave, as an inward possession to all, whether lord, bailiff or serf, the consciousness of mattering, of having, of inalienable spiritual right, even if not of physical fact, that place and freedom as a *member* of an organic structure in which social salvation lay. And it did this because it held out to him incorporation into an organism. For this reason its gospel appeared relevant. It spoke to men of becoming members or limbs of a Body: it offered them value as functional parts of the *Corpus Christi*. It knew what salvation, if it were to have any appeal, must show men the way to become—not individuals (that was not yet the social ideal), but dependent members of a whole. For such incorporation mass conversion was the adapted technique and the 'dependent' virtues of poverty, chastity ('yield your members servants to righteousness unto holiness') and obedience the ideal of perfection.

## 2. Capitalist society

Economically the basic fact here is the discovery of man's *independence* and power to control and manipulate nature for his own ends. The dominant concept, therefore, is that of independence, social salvation lying, not in becoming a dependent member, but in becoming an individual. It is as such that a man acquired value in capitalist society, the power to count and to make a difference. Rights were grounded in the individual, and pre-eminently in the individual as freeholder. These 'rights of man' were conceived as anterior to any social organization, whose origin and *raison d'être* rested in a voluntary association to ensure the inviolability of property and to remove any hindrances to absolute freedom of contract. To have 'a stake in the country', which was the basis of the franchise, meant to own capital or the means of production.[1] Power lay in economic independence. Every man's aim was to 'make good', so that he could stand on his own feet. The ethic of this society was individualistic and its virtues the exact opposite of those of dependence—business success rather than poverty earning the divine blessing, while self-expression and private enterprise superseded the mediaeval values of chastity and obedience. Social salvation meant, as the novels of Dickens so clearly illustrate, the rescuing of men to become individuals out of the mass of the proletariat who had no 'name' or identity, no power to count in society, because they had no capital.

[1] It is ironical that in Britain the last vestige of capitalist electoral privilege (the business premises vote) disappeared at the same time as, and with far less opposition than, the last vestige of feudal parliamentarianism (the representation of the universities as 'communes' of the realm).

At the Reformation the Church made the break which allowed it to speak of the divine redemption in terms that accorded with this redefinition of social salvation. While Protestantism defaulted disastrously in its gospel to society, its message of salvation for the individual was at all events relevant. The new religious ideal was, in Kierkegaard's words (who in his politics and ideological assumptions, if in nothing else, was so clearly a child of his age), 'to become an individual before God'. Protestantism afforded to every man a personal Saviour, and by its insistence that Christ died for him individually, assured him an eternal value in the sight of God. Be he a cipher in the political arithmetic of this age, he could confidently hope to be counted among the number of the elect. With this new ideal of salvation went inevitably an individualist piety and an individualist ethic; and on the radical wing of the Protestant movement, at any rate, the notion of a 'gathered Church' and of congregational autonomy superseded the *Una Sancta* of Catholicism. And the change of goal was accompanied by a change of technique. In place of mass conversion of serfs or outcastes to incorporation in a Body, was put the rescuing of individual souls, 'plucked from the burning' of the submerged classes to be given value and self-respect as brothers for whom Christ died.

### 3. *Socialized society*[1]

The features of this type of society are not yet finally clear, but certain definite things can be said about it. In an important sense it is a synthesis of the two previous types. Its basic economic reality is neither dependence nor independence, but *interdependence*. The days of *laissez-faire* are gone for ever, the elbow-room has disappeared in which a man could 'do what he liked with his

[1] A 'socialized' society is to be distinguished from a 'socialist' society. It is a matter of sheer economic fact that the world is moving into an ordering of society which, whatever its political complexion, is bound in large degree to be socialized. As opposed to this fact, socialism is a theory, or an ideology, produced by the change in society to explain it, justify it and speed it. In exactly the same way, the economic and political theories of Locke and Adam Smith, Tom Paine and Bentham were produced (albeit largely unconsciously) by the capitalist revolution to explain it, justify it and speed it.

own' without denying the same liberty to others. The brute fact of our economic interdependence in 'one world' is borne home upon us ever more pressingly. Neutrality and isolationism are becoming impossible. If we are to survive at all, it is clear that it can only be as 'members one of another', in the responsible freedom of a community where all care for each and each works for all. The line between private and public is blurring. It is the age of planning, of the social service state and corporate ownership. While the virtues of dependence and obedience are at a discount and the standards of individual morality are crumbling, yet the consciousness of social interdependence and mutual responsibility has undoubtedly been strengthened. In place of the feudal thesis of slavish dependence and the capitalist antithesis of selfish independence, the ideal is of a freedom found in the reciprocity of community service.

But this ideal is threatened by a slavery more terrible, because more totalitarian, than that which hung over either of the other two types of society. Never was social salvation a more urgent postulate than it is for modern man. But this salvation is neither from the political submergence of the outcaste, the slave and the serf to membership of the *Corpus*, nor from the economic submergence of the industrial proletariat to self-conscious individuality. Political and economic democracy have in principle been attained. But such democracy may still leave a man with the frustrating realization that he has no value in his society, no power to count or make significant difference to it. Only too easily may he be drowned in the mass, swallowed up in impersonality. Redemption for him means being released to become a person —not an individual, because in independence he is powerless in face of the all-controlling State—but a person, who may find rather than lose himself in the interdependence of the community. The 'they' depersonalizes: a man achieves personality, or is redeemed to it, when he discovers himself addressed and treated as a 'thou' and can respond in the same way in his relationships to others. The content of social salvation for the modern man is to discover himself as a person, as one who freely chooses interdependence, because his **nature** is to be made for others, rather than one who is engulfed in it because the pressures of his age demand it.

The Church's chance of claiming the socialized society upon which we are entering depends on whether it can speak its gospel of redemption in terms of this new content of social salvation. Can it show men that through Christianity, and through Christianity alone, they can truly become persons, as mediaeval Catholicism held out to them the goal of incorporation in a Body and reformation Protestantism the possibility of becoming individuals before God?

If it is to achieve this it will need to re-examine its evangelistic method. It is clear that neither mass conversion nor the saving of a man out of and apart from his environment is nowadays possible or desirable. It is not desirable because neither technique treats him as a person or builds him into one: it is not possible because economically and socially it is only as a person and to become a person that today he can be saved if he is to be saved at all. This means that conversion must be, through and through, a community affair. For a man becomes a person when he discovers himself in the I-Thou relation of community, and in actual experience grasps with the total response of his being that he has been made for, and has his centre in, other persons.

This means a rethinking, not only of the technique of evangelism, but also of its goal—the Church. It is impossible to rest either with the mediaeval interpretation of the Church as the *Corpus Christi*, which precedes the individual and into which he is simply grafted, or with the later Protestant conception of it as the gathered congregation, which exists only as the result of an aggregation of individuals. The terms person and community are correlative. One cannot be prior to the other, because persons exist only in community and community means nothing more than persons being persons. For some indication of the lines along which this redefinition of the Church must be made, one may refer to Canon T. O. Wedel's striking book, *The Coming Great Church*.

Mention of this book, steeped as it is in the new biblical theology, may serve to dispel the fears that such a reinterpretation means a trimming of the gospel to the requirements of an alien sociology. It is in fact precisely those who have made the return to the Bible and rediscovered the centrality of God's kingdom and fellowship, the *basileia* and the *koinonia*, who have most to offer to this generation. Indeed it is surely a profound confirmation of the working of the grace and power of God that, despite the ever-mounting sin of man, the dialectic of economic forces should have produced a series of societies in which the definition of social salvation comes to approximate, through thesis, antithesis and synthesis, more closely to the true content of eternal salvation. The social order at present emerging may contain within it potentialities of destruction and dehumanization of which any previous order was incapable. On the other hand, it must be recognized that the concepts of community, personality, freedom, responsiblity and morality demanded as the content of salvation within it are in fact closer to the Christian definition of these things than those demanded either by pre-scientific or by capitalist society. Moreover, if God gave to the Church so to interpret its gospel of salvation as to fulfil both the one-sided social ideals of incorporation and of individualism, then surely he may be trusted to empower his followers to present it now, when society demands it, in what can be the fully Christian terms of redemption to personal community.

But while eternal salvation has to be presented in tems of the content of social salvation to be relevrnt, the two are, of course, never identical. The Church must always declare that the social ideal is not self-sufficient: it must relate it to an ultimate responsibility to, and fulfilment in, God, and assert that in fact it can be attained only as a by-product of this further relation. It has to preach divine salvation in terms, indeed, of the peculiar salvation relevant to the order of society to which it speaks, but it has to proclaim that salvation as something that gains its relevance, not from society, but from God. Through the gospel men must be led to discover their lives to be meaningful in society, but yet as meaningless apart from God.

The righteous, the socially saved, do not want this gospel: it is foolishness to them. It is to the socially outcaste, submerged and depersonalized, that the word of the Cross first comes with power. It offers them the true caste, individuality and personality —but only by One who is crucified by caste, outlawed and extinguished by society. In St Paul's paradox, in order to establish the divine righteousness (salvation from the hand of God), the gospel of the Cross destroys the righteousness of the Law (self-sufficient social salvation)—only to confirm the Law, by affording, as a by-product, genuine salvation in society. The gospel *does* give men meaning and fulfilment in society, and unless it is preached in terms of the particular content of this social salvation it becomes irrelevant; but it tells them that this is to be had, not by seeking it, but by losing it, not by striving and works, but by faith and grace. 'Seek ye first the kingdom of God and his righteousness, and all these things shall be added unto you.'

# CHAPTER THREE

# Matter, Power, and Liturgy[1]

## 1. MATTER

MATERIALISM AT HOME and power politics abroad: a concern for these twin evils of our time is not confined to the jeremiads of the pious. Every thinking person can see that they have it in them to bring about slow death or the sudden destruction of everything for which we stand. 'The walls of gold entomb us, the swords of scorn divide,' wrote G. K. Chesterton over fifty years ago. And nothing which has happened since indicates that we know any more how to use matter or power in such a way that they will not corrupt us from within or destroy us from without. All that has happened is that the problem has been blown up to proportions that we can now neither comprehend nor control.

It is alarming enough in this situation that those who claim to have control—or at any rate have access to the switches—should be feeling around and lunging about for all the world like players engaged in blind man's buff. 'Our earthly rulers falter, our people drift and die.' The complacency and lack of alternative with which we look on at this macabre performance is frightening. But quite as disturbing is the fact that the Christian Church and Christian theologians seem to be showing practically no signs of 'engagement' at this point at all. Of all that is pouring out from our theological presses and our pulpits, how much is really attempting to come to grips with these great material and power-political problems in which our civilization is locked? How much of it is giving any serious consideration to what the *Christian* doctrine of matter and power might be? It is easy to agree that

[1] The Reinicker Lectures, delivered at the Episcopal Theological Seminary, Alexandria, Virginia, May 1958.

'materialism' is a 'bad thing'; but what is the Christian understanding and use of matter? It has become a commonplace that
'all power corrupts, and absolute power corrupts absolutely'; but
where do we tell people to go from there?

There is indeed one strain in Christian thinking—the ascetic
and the pacifist—which at least gives a certain answer: 'We must
give up matter, we must renounce power'. But you can do that
only by going out of the world, partial and symbolic as your
withdrawal from it is bound to be. What are we to say to the man
who feels no such call, who knows he must serve his God and
generation within the structures of this world, creating the wealth
that entombs us, perfecting the missiles to divide and blow us to
pieces? And, more generally, what guidance are we giving to the
mass of lay men and women who do not know what to think,
who are certainly not going to contract out of the material order
or the power situation, and for whom indeed it would be irre-
sponsible to do so, since they have commitments, and often
important responsibilities, within it?

I do not pretend to supply the answer to these questions in
three short lectures; and indeed I am not going to try. I should
like to address myself to a prior task—not to answer the ethical
questions, so much as to look to the foundations in the Bible and
in the life of the Christian community on which alone these
answers can be built. In the first lecture, I shall consider the basic
Christian doctrine of matter, enquiring how Christianity under-
stands the meaning and destiny in God's purpose of this material
order. In the second, I shall try to do the same thing for the
Christian doctrine of power. In the third, I want to attempt
something rather different. This is to draw out the implications
for the social and the material order of what Christains actually
*do* with matter in the central action of their common life, or,
rather, of what Christ does with it. For, like Marxists, Christians
are concerned with understanding the world primarily in order
to change it. But, unlike Marxists, they look for the bringing
about of this change, not in the first instance to their own actions,
but to what God in Christ has done, is doing, and will do about
it. To discuss what Christians should do except in the light and

in the power of this divine act is to invite them, in St Paul's words, to 'war according to the flesh,' to enter the conflict, that is, with the outlook and resources of the world—to which all too soon they will then be conformed.

Nowhere in the whole field of Christian thought is the call to 'be transformed in the renewing of your minds' more necessary or more difficult, at no point of our engagement is it harder to be in the world without being of it. We are not in the lump, and we are too much in it, at the same time. And it is this false relationship of our Christian *living* to the world of matter and power which stunts and distorts our thinking about them. The purification of our theology at this point is likely to proceed only from the purification of our practical relationships, from an existential rediscovery of what it means to '*be* the Church' within the world in which we are set. Only out of an actual community which has made that recovery—and not out of a set of lectures—can we hope to win the guidance that our business man and our trades unionist, our atomic physicist, and indeed every Christian layman, has the right to expect from the Church.

With that introduction let me plunge straight into my first theme—the Christian doctrine of matter.

'I believe in one God, the Father Almighty, Maker of heaven and earth, and of all things visible and invisible.' Those words may seem perhaps a rather long-winded way of saying that God created everything. But they were put into the Nicene Creed for a quite deliberate reason. They were to mark Christianity off once and for all from the competing -ologies and -isms of that age, and of every age, which said that God was to be discovered in the world of spirit but had no connection with matter, which was evil, unreal, or unimportant. The typical view of man and of the world against which Christianity had to establish itself in the Graeco-Roman world can be summed up in the Platonic pun: *soma sema*, the body is a tomb; the whole vast nexus of matter and history is the prison-house of the soul, whose divine destiny is to be achieved only by release from it into the invisible, timeless order of spirit.

B

Against this the biblical world-view is uncompromising. Its doctrine of creation is not the Greek notion of spirit trying to impose form or design on an intractable porridgey mass of matter, for which it is not responsible. It asserts that God made *everything*, visible and invisible alike, matter and spirit; and, behold, it was very good. The Bible then goes on to say (and this is what the historical books and the Prophets are about) that this creator God is to be met and known not in a flight from history, but through obedience to facts and events—physical facts, economic facts, political and international events. And finally, at the very centre of the biblical record, stands the assertion that 'the Word was made flesh', in which, as it were, God said to men: 'If you want spirit you must have matter; there is no other way to the Father'. Indeed, Christianity stands or falls by the sacramental principle, that matter and spirit are not separate or antithetical; that one is not to be found by turning away from the other, but in, through and under it. The whole robe of creation is like shot silk, matter and spirit, as, to quote Bismarck of all people, 'the garment of God rustles through events'.[1]

It is because Christianity has thus dared to take the body of history seriously, that it is within Christian civilization alone that any view of progress has arisen. Again, it is because Christianity has refused to view matter as irrational but seen in it the *logos*, the order and reason of God, that it is within Christian civilization that science has burgeoned. In a post-Christian age these things need occasionally to be said.

It was William Temple who made the now famous remark that Christianity is 'the most avowedly materialist of all the great religions'. Not so well known is his other observation, of Marxist dialectical materialism, that 'its own dialectic will destroy its character as materialist'.[2] There is no more facile analysis than to conclude that, while Communism is 'materialist', Christianity is 'spiritual', and that is that. Christianity is not spiritual in the

---

[1] Cited by H. Butterfield, *Christianity and History*, p. 100: 'The statesman must try and reach for the hem when he hears the garment of God rustling through events'.

[2] *Nature, Man and God*, p. 488.

sense that it denies matter, nor if you really study Marxism, will you find it denies spirit. The Russian Orthodox philosopher Nicolas Berdyaev, who began as a Communist, expressed the truth common to both of them at their best when he wrote: 'Bread for myself is a material problem: bread for other people is a spiritual problem'. That, I believe, is a profound remark and bears much pondering. It is precisely because nineteenth century Christianity (and much twentieth-century Christianity) held that religion and morals for other people was alone the spiritual problem that God found Communism necessary, and still does.

For, despite all that is in the Bible, Christians have been extraordinarily reluctant to assert in practice that the body, just as much as the soul, is 'for the Lord'. Historically Christianity has always felt more at home with an idealist than with an empiricist or materialist philosophy. Indeed, many Christians would be surprised to be told that there was any such thing as a Christian doctrine of matter and hard put to it to say what it was. Much of our trouble has been that the Church has had no thought-out doctrine of matter. Christians always tend to be uncomfortable at this point, and the Church's thinking has swung rather aimlessly between two poles. There are those, on the one hand, who would stress the undoubted biblical emphasis that here we have no abiding city, that man does not live by bread alone, that the things that are seen are not the things that are eternal. On the other hand, there are those who would stress what they believe to be the equally biblical emphasis of concern for the whole man, body, mind and spirit, declaring with the Prophets that God cares about sewers as much as sanctuaries, for politics as much as prayer.

Where, between these two, lies the true Christian doctrine of matter?

Let us start with a passage from St Paul, in I Cor. 6.12-20, which poses the issue as clearly as any. The Apostle is facing a problem that was focussed, if possible, even more sharply in Corinth than it is for us. In that highly materialistic city 'sex' filled the eye, and received a valuation which even in the twentieth century might raise a few eyebrows. In this situation those who were 'spiritual' refused this valuation; they set a low estimate on the things of the body. Surely, they assumed, Christianity must side with them. What does St Paul say?

He begins apparently by agreeing: 'Food is for the belly and the belly for food—and God will destroy the one with the other'. In other words, these things are here today, gone tomorrow; they have no abiding value. But then he goes on: 'But the body is not for fornication, but for the Lord; and the Lord for the body: and God both raised the Lord, and will raise us up through his power'.

It is in this apparently contradictory valuation between 'the belly' and 'the body' that the clue to the Christian doctrine of matter is to be found. It is the same distinction that St Paul draws elsewhere between 'the flesh' and 'the body'. Now this is a difficult distinction for us, because we think of the flesh as *part* of the body—as when we say that a man is made up of flesh and bones, or of flesh and spirit. But this is not how St Paul normally uses the words.[1] When he speaks of 'flesh' he begins from the same point as the Old Testament writers when they spoke of 'all flesh' as grass, by which they meant 'all men', not some part of man's being, but the whole of human life bound up in solidarity with nature. Yet when the biblical writers describe man as 'flesh' it is always from a particular point of view, with a particular nuance. Man as 'flesh' indicates man in his difference and distance from God. *God* is spirit, God is life-giving power: *man* is flesh—weak, transient and mortal. To speak of man as 'flesh' is the biblical way of saying that man has no enduring vitality in himself, that like the rest of the natural creation he is subject to dissolution and decay. 'Flesh' indeed designates more than man as a mere animal. It includes also what distinguishes history from nature. All the highest products of human culture and civilization, all that we should call the things of the mind and spirit, are 'flesh'. The Bible speaks of flesh '*and all the glory thereof*'—and it has a real glory. But it is the glory of the flower that fades. For the Bible, man's ideas and ideals are just as much by-products of the material order as they are for Marx: 'Man returns to his dust, and then all his thoughts perish'.

[1] For a fuller treatment of this and other themes in this lecture I would refer to my book *The Body*.

This is the basis for that estimate of matter in Christianity which sits loose to all material things. The outward man is decaying day by day; we have here no abiding city; a man's life consists not in the abundance of the things that he possesses. This estimate is an essential part of Christian doctrine and an essential element in Christian preaching, against the materialism of this and every age. But it is an element which in the course of Christian history has been given a false twist by association with a Greek view of the world, with its notion, completely alien to the Bible, that matter is in itself evil or illusory.

But while the Bible insists that all matter and all human life is 'flesh', yet this is not its last word. St Paul expresses this in the passage I quoted by saying that whereas 'the belly' and everything it represents is going, as we say, 'the way of all flesh', 'the body' is 'for the Lord'. Again, it is important to insist that by 'the body' he is not meaning another *part* of human nature, the 'higher' or more spiritual part, as opposed to the physical. In fact, as I said, he is talking about sex, and in the immediate context he is actually discussing the most crudely physical relationship of all, a man's union with a prostitute. Here above all he might be expected to apply the principle 'meats for the belly and the belly for meats'. And this is precisely what his 'spiritual' friends in Corinth expected him to say: such a relationship belongs simply to the realm of 'flesh'; it has no eternal significance. But St Paul refuses to confine it to this level, though like all else it has indeed to be judged at this level. He insists that there is also another level, another view-point, from which sex, like the whole of human life, must be assessed. And it is this that he designates by the word 'body'.

Once again, 'the body' is co-extensive with 'the flesh': in fact, for a great many purposes the two words are interchangeable. It describes not a different set of relationships, but the same solidarity of human existence, now looked at, however, not in its difference and distance *from* God, but as created and destined *for* God. 'The body is not for fornication, *but for the Lord*'. That is to say, the destiny for which it exists is not, like that of 'flesh', decay and death, but relationship with the eternal God. Man, matter, thus considered wears a very different aspect and demands a very different valuation. For every relationship, however material, therewith takes on eternal significance and is charged with eternal consequence. However trivial, however purely physical, everything a man does 'in the body' is not to be judged merely by the fact that this physical collocation of atoms will soon be dispersed as if it had never been. For what he does is being built into an order of reality, a structure of relationships, which does not come to an end even with death.

As we now know it, indeed, the solidarity of human existence, even as 'body', *is* a solidarity doomed to frustration and death. 'Who shall deliver me,' cries St Paul, 'from this body of death?' (Rom. 7.24). But death is its doom, not its destiny. It is indeed natural for flesh to decay and die: it is profoundly unnatural for the body of creation, made for God, to be subjected to the ends simply of flesh. Paul speaks of it as being subjected to 'futility' (Rom. 8.20), to what frustrates its true nature.

And yet at the same time he speaks of the *redemption* of this body. The central fact of the Christian message is not simply that the body is 'for the Lord'—that by itself would merely remind us of our frustration—but, as he at once goes on, that the Lord is 'for the body'. He, the Lord, has identified himself with it, sunk himself in it. 'And God both raised the Lord, and will raise us up through his power'. That is the promise to man, to the whole of creation, as body. St Paul never speaks of the resurrection of the flesh. But he does speak of the resurrection of the body. The hope of creation is to be delivered from its present bondage to decay, and through Christ to share in the resurrection order of life, the new heaven and the new earth. And man is chosen to be the first fruits of this new creation. It is through man that creation failed to achieve its proper relationship with God; it is through man, the priest of nature, that the whole body of creation must ultimately be restored to that eternal destiny for which originally it was called into being.

The resurrection of the body! We cannot understand the Christian doctrine of matter without it. And yet it would doubtless seem to most people a concept utterly irrelevant to the ordinary business of Christian living in this material world. Normally it occupies their minds only when they or their loved ones take their leave from it. Perhaps, therefore, you will bear with me if I spend a little time trying to set this doctrine in its proper proportions and correct some of the misconceptions with which for all of us it has come to be associated.

In the first place, it has nothing to do with the resuscitation of corpses or the recomposition of dead matter—a doctrine historically to be distinguished as 'the resurrection of the flesh' and, as I said, as repugnant to Scripture as it is to reason. St Paul makes it clear that it is not this body which is resuscitated, as his Rabbinic opponents supposed and as a good deal of unthinking resistance to cremation still tacitly assumes. Indeed, if it did not have the effect of fixing our thinking about this doctrine still further upon the moment of death, one might use it as the text for a number of pregnant comments on contemporary funeralia and in particular upon that remarkable, and expensive, reverence for the corpse which manages to unite American and Soviet materialism in death if not in life!

The second misconception about the resurrection of the body is that Christianity asserts this doctrine in order to safeguard our continuing survival as individual persons, as against any idea of re-absorption such as is found in Hinduism or Buddhism. Of course, the Christian gospel is absolutely clear that our eternal destiny consists in an utterly personal and inalienable relationship to God in the communion of saints. But, biblically speaking, this is not what 'the resurrection of the *body*' is concerned to safeguard or to stress. On the contrary, it is emphasizing this destiny not as something irreplaceably individual, but as something inescapably corporate. As against the idea of the immortality of the soul (itself fondly imagined to be a cardinal Christian doctrine), it affirms that no one of us can achieve his destiny in isolation from his neighbour, nor indeed from the whole of the rest of creation. For 'the body', to the Hebrew way of thinking, is the symbol of solidarity, not, as it has been in Greek and Western thought, the principle of individuation. It is what binds man together in the bundle of life, not what marks off or isolates one man from the next. And that is why the New Testament connects the resurrection of the body, not with the moment of the individual's death, but with *the last day*, when all the relationships of nature and history shall finally have been knit up, no longer in their present solidarity of sin and death, but into the new solidarity of life, the body of Christ's glory.

This brings us again to the third and perhaps most persistent misunderstanding, that the resurrection of the body is all to do with the moment of death. That is impressed upon our minds, no doubt, by the reading of I Corinthians 15 at funerals. But that classic chapter revolves around two points only, the third day and the last day; and in the resurrection of the body St Paul is clearly describing something which is to take place, as he puts it, at 'the last trump', that is, at the consummation of history. But more important even than the fact that the putting on of the new body is not, and cannot be, *completed* at death is the fact that it is not *begun* at death. It is begun at Baptism—when by entering the body of Christ a man's life ceases to be bound up simply with the old mortality, and from then on starts to grow into that resurrection order of existence which will one day be the only one. The moment of death has no significance for this putting on of the new: it has no place in the calendar of the new life. But it is a decisive stage in the stripping off of the old; for it lays bare just how much of a man's life has in fact been rebuilt into that new set of relationships, that new body, in Christ, which, though invisible, alone is eternal in the heavens.

Having thus tried to set aside some of the misunderstandings, let me now attempt to state positively the doctrine of the resurrection of the body, and its significance for the Christian understanding of matter.

The ultimate destiny of all creation, according to the New Testament, is to be transformed from being merely a natural body to becoming a spiritual body, an organic whole, that is to say, perfectly reflecting and expressing the Spirit of him who made it. And the means by which God has chosen to bring this about is to introduce into the body of this world, into its lovelessness, its cruelties, its materialism, its hopelessness, a cell of that new life of which eventually all will be composed. The only perfect specimen of this life that has yet appeared is the man Christ Jesus, the first representative of God's new creation within the old. But this, since the Resurrection, is no isolated, individual cell. Thenceforth, the body of Christ is a corporate reality, recreating the old around it by drawing into its new life those whose being has hitherto been bound up in the solidarity of sin and death. This new organism has still, within this world, much of the outward appearance of the old. Yet it contains within it that life-giving Spirit, that element of the age to come, which must ultimately reduce and transform all things. St Paul can even say that those thus endowed and quickened have been 'glorified' (Rom. 8.30), that they are transparent, in however small degree, with the resurrection quality that one day all life must wear. Such is the Church, the body of Christ, that 'thing of glory', as it is described in Eph. 5.27. It is set within this world by God to be, in St James's words, 'a kind of first fruits of his creatures' (Jas. 1.18), the pledge, and at the same time the agent, of all creation's destiny. Into this resurrection body of history we are brought at Baptism; of it we partake in the Eucharist; into it we are being transformed, from glory to glory, by the power of the Spirit; and to it we trust finally to be conformed, as we grow up in all things into Christ, who shall change our lowly body to be like his glorious body, by the power which enables him to subject all things to himself.

That is the end picture. But meanwhile it must control all our commitments within this material order. The Christian knows that this world is 'flesh': he will not lose his heart to it nor lay up treasure within it, for that is to live, as St Paul puts it, 'according to the flesh', allowing the aspect of the world as flesh to determine one's whole horizon and outlook. And 'the mind of the flesh', the nearest New Testament equivalent to 'materialism', is death (Rom. 8.6): for the end of the flesh is corruption, and to try to find one's whole life within it is to embrace death as one's destiny.

But, without going out of this world, and without being one whit less concerned for bread because he knows better than anyone that man cannot live by bread alone, the Christian is called to take his part within that new body whose relationships are eternal in the heavens. It is not a body in heaven, for which he departs, so much as a body *from* heaven, a new God-given structure of existence which has already begun to interpenetrate and transform this one, and into which one day all nature and all history must be taken up and restored.

'The body is for the Lord': it is necessary to say this when the collectives and giant power corporations of the modern world seem well-nigh demonic. They are still created by God and for God. The Christian must affirm them. But he is under no illusion that the body of existence as we now know it is good: it is a solidarity which corrupts community, frustrates freedom, and destroys the bodies and souls of men. For it is a body of death. But 'the Lord is for the body', this body. For the rescue of an immortal soul one might even dare to die; but for this seamy, smoky mass of sin and death who could lose his heart or give his life? Yet the Christian gospel is that in Christ God did lose his heart precisely for this and submitted himself to live in its solidarities and transform it by his death. 'And God raised the Lord, and will also raise us up by his power. Do you not know that your bodies are members of Christ? . . . You are not your own; you were bought with a price. So glorify God in your body.' There, in briefest compass, is the whole Christian doctrine of matter, first in the indicative and then in the imperative.

What that imperative means it is not, as I said, my present purpose to pursue. What it involves to 'glorify God *in* your body' —in, rather than out of, the solidarities of this world order—is indeed the central question of Christian social ethics. All that I have tried to do in this lecture is to suggest that the answer to that question cannot be found except in relation to the whole Christian understanding of *the resurrection body*. This indeed is an eschatological reality, something that belongs to the last time. But it is also a present reality, within the body of Christ. It is in the Church that matter is redeemed, and above all at the point at which Christ still says over this sinful secular order of ours, represented in that of it which we will offer to him, '*This* is *my body*'. To the implications of that for our thinking and practice I shall return in my third lecture.

## 2. POWER

THE CHRISTIAN DOCTRINE of power is but an extension of its doctrine of matter. For all power ultimately, as atomic power reminds us most vividly, is a function of matter—or perhaps it would be truer to modern physics to say that matter is itself power, energy. In any case, our involvement in power and power relationships is simply part of our being in the world. From the moment we are born, we enter a vast and interlocking structure of power relationships, an unbroken continuum linking our lives at one end with the power that moves the sun and moon and other stars and at the other with the power of our mother's love. In between lie all the complexes of social and industrial, economic and military power, which are reflected in every freedom we exercise and every control we obey. All relationships, even the most personal ones between husband and wife, parents and children, involve the adjustment and sublimation of power. A view of the world and an ethic which does not come to terms in a realistic way with power can be both futile and dangerous. But it is true, I suspect again, that most Christians would scarcely be aware that there was such a thing as a Christian doctrine of power. And it is in their assessment of power and power situations that Christians tend to be most unrealistic and sloppy in their moral thinking. In practice, they are usually a good deal more hard headed, but often only at the expense of failing to be distinctively Christian.

Here, as with matter, the first thing that the Christian has to assert is that, in the words of the Psalmist, 'power belongs to God' (Ps. 62.11). Power is part of the primordial structure of creation that God saw and, behold, it was very good. And part at least of what it means for man to be made in the image of God is that he is not merely, like the rest of creation, subject to this power structure, but, under God, responsible for it: he is to subdue the earth and share God's dominion over it. Moreover, the exercise of power over other men—which is where the crux of the moral problem lies—is also part of the divinely ordained structure of life within this world. 'For there is no authority except from God, and those that exist have been instituted by God. Therefore he who resists the authorities resists what God has appointed' (Rom. 13.1f.). This is not to say that the state, the ultimate repository of this power, may not, like the Church, become apostate: the New Testament fully allows for this. But the very notion of apostasy presupposes a positive divine ordinance from which to fall away.

All this may sound obvious enough. But in practice so used are we to the dogma—and indeed to the experience—that 'all power tends to corrupt' (Lord Acton did not say, as he is regularly quoted, that 'all power corrupts', as if this were something inevitable), that most people think instinctively—and the more pious they are the more inclined they are to think it—that power is in itself something evil and sub-Christian. This comes out very clearly in the use of the term 'power politics' for the sort of politics of which we disapprove, the implication being that the sort of politics we are engaged in is not 'power' politics. Yet, of course, all politics is of its very nature power politics, since its essential function is the adjustment of power relationships. If war is the continuation of politics by other means, politics is the resolution of power situations short of war. Politics is never concerned with the abolition of power, but with harnessing power to law, with putting might behind right. Yet there are large numbers of good and religious people who genuinely suppose that the characteristically Christian attitude in politics consists in the renunciation of power and that the distinctive contribution of Christianity to politics is one that by-passes power —namely, the fostering of personal relationships *despite and across* the lines of power (e.g. getting trade unionists and management to love one another). There are many Christians who, if they do not actually think that power belongs to the devil, at least do not act very conspicuously as though it belonged to God.

Now the first step in Christian realism is to recognize that, in what Dr Emil Brunner has called 'the world of systems' (everywhere, that is, except in the realm of pure personal dealing at the individual level), it is not primarily for the abolition of power that the Christian must take his stand. Any pacificism, for instance, that enters the political field with that bias must, I think, be condemned as heretical. The Christian is no more committed to the abolition or renunciation of power for its own sake than he is to the abolition or renunciation of matter for its own sake: that is Manichaeism not Christianity. The Christian enters politics, rather in order to see that power is placed behind right. In other words, he is not concerned in this field primarily for the ends of *love*, for bringing into being that relationship of *agape* where nature is transcended in grace, where the realities of power—of what is due, of what can be insisted on and enforced—become irrelevant. In politics he must take his stand, not for the renunciation of power in love, but for the subordination of power to justice.

But so accustomed are we to regarding justice simply as a second-best to love—and, from the point of view of the distinctive mission of *the Church*, to establish relationships of justice is *not* its primary task—that many Christians react at this point in one of two illegitimate ways. *Either* they recognize that politics *is* concerned with justice and not with love, and conclude therefore that this is not the Church's job and that Christians should keep out of politics. *Or* they refuse to recognize that politics is concerned with justice, and go into it as if the Christian contribution were to inject into it a bit more love. This may take the form of working for the abolition of power, in the first instance, of course, of some particularly terrible manifestation of power, like the H-bomb, but without any realistic appraisal of how this particular manifestation of power is interlocked with every other manifestation of power. Or, more generally, it takes the form of assuming that a Christian goes into politics to 'make it a bit more Christian'. By this is meant to get people to love each other more and not to stand so much upon their rights—in other words, again, to waive power. Now more of this self-renouncing *agape*, the love of the Cross, is a desperately desirable thing; and the leavening of all of life by it is indeed the primary aim of the Church's mission. But it is not the primary aim of politics, and

Christians will rightly earn the discredit of the world if they go into politics thinking that it is. For within politics justice is not an inferior substitute for love, what you settle for if you cannot persuade people to be loving: it is the current coin of love, love's only legal tender, as Brunner calls it,[1] within the world of systems. If your aim is love for your neighbour, then the only way in which you can give effect to it *within this setting* (and, of course, your neighbour is not wholly contained within this setting) is by working for justice. If you go into politics with anything else as your primary object, then you will only succeed in being unrealistic, ineffectual, and very soon disillusioned.

This is a truth which I suspect has still hardly begun to penetrate the general consciousness of the Church; and for this reason perhaps I may be allowed to state it again in different words, this time in those of William Temple. I quote from the very significant little pamphlet which was originally written as a supplement to *The Christian News-Letter* just before his death, called *What Christians Stand for in the Secular World*. He is emphasizing what I have just been saying that the Christian's concern for neighbour at this point, and therefore for God and his kingdom, is not to be expressed primarily as love, as the establishment of pure personal dealing. 'Associations', he said, 'cannot love one another; a trade union cannot love an employers' federation, nor can one national State love another'. The members of one may love the members of the other so far as opportunities of intercourse allow. That will help in negotiations; but it will not solve the problem of the relationships between the two groups. Consequently, the relevance of Christianity in these spheres is quite different from what many Christians suppose it to be. Christian charity manifests itself in the temporal order as a supernatural discernment of, and adhesion to, *justice* in relation to the equilibrium of power. . . . It is precisely fellowship or human love, with which too often Christian charity is mistakenly equated, that is not seriously relevant in that sphere. When the two are identified, it is just those who are most honest and realistic in their thinking and practice that are apt to be repelled from Christianity.'[2]

[1] *Justice and the Social Order*, p. 116.    [2] *Op. cit.*, pp. 14f.

The reduction of every political and economic problem to a simple *moral* issue is a very great heresy, the basic heresy, from a Christian point of view, of Moral Rearmament. Let me quote again, this time from the man of our own time who has given more thought than anyone else to the relevance of Christianity in this field, Professor Reinhold Niebuhr. 'The moral achievement of individual good-will is not a substitute for the mechanisms of social control. It may perfect and purify, but it cannot create basic justice. . . . The health of a social organism depends upon the adequacy of its social structure as much as does the health of the body upon the biochemical processes. No degree of goodwill alone can cure a deficiency in glandular secretions; and no moral idealism can overcome a basic mechanical defect in the social structure.'[1] To act as though it could is to ignore the physical basis of life in the spirit. It is yet another form of the old Manichaean heresy, that matter, if not evil, is at any rate unreal, that the basic realities of power, like the physical structure of the body, can be ignored, and every problem solved simply at the moral level. Only too frequently, says Niebuhr again, has Christianity been identified with 'the monotonous reiteration of the pious hope that people might be good and loving, in which case all the nasty business of politics could be dispensed with'.[2]

This same basic illusion is also to be seen in the deprecation of force or coercion in political action—for instance, in middle-class abhorrence of strikes. Obviously social violence is a very great evil and ought to be eliminated wherever possible. But that is precisely what politics, as opposed to war, is concerned to achieve. It does this, however, not by disavowing force, but by achieving such a combination of equity and power that disturbance of it is both unprovoked and unprofitable. To quote Niebuhr again, 'The very essence of politics is the achievement of justice through equilibria of power. A balance of power is not conflict; but a tension between opposing forces underlies it. Where there is tension there is potential conflict, and where there is conflict there is potential violence. A responsible relationship to the political order, therefore, makes an unqualified disavowal of

[1] *An Interpretation of Christian Ethics*, p. 192.    [2] *Op. cit.*, p. 187.

violence impossible. There may always be crises in which the cause of justice will have to be defended against those who will attempt its violent destruction.'[1]

It is at this point that we encounter what, as it seems to me, is the real crux of our contemporary problem—and that is the interdependence of all power. One cannot disavow power, or the decisive form of power, without undermining the whole structure upon which justice rests. And that becomes ever more true in a world where, like peace, power is indivisible. A Quaker friend once said to me, 'I believe in democracy, but I don't believe in defending it by force.' We can all see what she meant and sympathize with it. But the very possibility of democracy, and the framework of law, freedom and justice it provides, rests upon a most stupendous balance of force, by which it is continuously being defended. Leaving out of all account the *internal* equilibrium of power which democracy presupposes, depending in the last resort upon the militia in the background, the very survival of western democracy since the War has rested ultimately on the threat of the atomic and now the hydrogen bomb. It has been and is preserved at all only within this terrible ring of steel. That is part of the inescapable agony of our time—for pacifists and non-pacifists alike.

It is this interrelationship of all power which for me makes the pacifist issue so much more complex than most pacifists I have met appear to allow, and why every time I am driven to the brink of pacifism I am pushed back—by the pacifists. On the one hand, there seems no escape from the thought, which can never be far from anyone of us, that modern war with all it entails is *so* evil that there are no imaginable circumstances in which it could be the lesser of two evils. And I have the greatest possible sympathy and respect for those who say, 'Here is something, whatever the consequences, to which as a Christian I cannot be party'. And perhaps that is where one should stop: 'So help me God, I can no other.'

But the trouble is that I find I cannot stop there. If it were merely a matter of other theoretical considerations, they could

[1] *Op. cit.*, p. 200.

perhaps be dismissed, however weighty, because in this case nothing could outweigh what is in the other scale. And if I were in the position of the early Christians, and still indeed of most Christians in the world today, of simply being at the receiving end of power, of being responsible to it but not also responsible for it, that is probably where the matter *would* stop. My difficulty begins when I ask myself just what is the next practical step in the situation in which we ourselves are, of Christian citizens with a responsibility for the use of power from which we cannot simply abdicate, or which, if we do abdicate, must necessarily be carried by non-Christians.

If it were a question simply of joining a crusade to 'ban the bomb' or even to 'outlaw war', as one would go about a campaign to wipe out leprosy or abolish cancer, it would be relatively easy. But supposing one wants, with any realistic appreciation of the power structure, to turn this into a practical *political* programme, what does one do?

Let me take an illustration from recent English politics, which I believe to be instructive. It was at the time when Britain decided to go ahead and manufacture its own hydrogen bomb. Sir Richard Acland, a keen and intelligent Anglican layman, resigned his seat as Labour Member of Parliament for Gravesend in order to force an election on this issue. It was a brave gesture, and indeed I believe that on the narrow issue he will be seen to have been right—that purely on the political level, this way of trying to remain master in our own house was for Britain a serious miscalculation (and has since proved a disastrous example)—though in face of the policy of the United States Government on atomic secrets at the time when the decision was taken, I am not prepared to throw stones at those who had the terrible responsibility of making it. But whether it was right or wrong as a political calculation is, for our present purpose, irrelevant. So too is the fact that Sir Richard polled only a fraction of the votes in a constituency where hitherto he had consistently increased his majority (though I am not so sure that it *is* entirely irrelevant if we are really concerned with how to stop this thing in the next ten years, which is all we may have; for what people will vote for is highly relevant). But the real lesson, for me, of this incident is the dilemma it poses for any political action of this kind. I remember discussing it at the time with a keen Christian pacifist who was also deeply involved in Labour city politics—the first person one would have thought to be sympathetic. And so, of course, he was. But he said, in effect, *C'est magnifique, mais ce n'est pas la politique*!

As a protest it *was* magnificent. And if it were simply a case of saying, 'No hydrogen bomb: we will have other kinds of nuclear weapons but not this', that would have been a calculated political risk, and probably a shrewd one. But no pacifist, except as a matter of temporary tactics, could take that position. The very least he is committed to is the renunciation of all nuclear weapons —and not only British ones, but the right to let the United States use them from British bases. And therewith he is committed to the dismantling of NATO and the whole power structure and policy of containment upon which the western world has rested since the War. And you cannot put up for Parliament and say, 'That little detail apart, I stand for the Labour party programme' —or for any other party programme. At least you can say it, and you might even get elected, and you might spend your time battling for all the admirable causes with which a person like Sir Richard Acland has associated himself—War on Want, the abolition of capital punishment, and so on. But you will be able to do it only because everyone else is preserving the ring of steel within which your programme of reform has any immediate validity. And what is true of the member of Parliament is true in lesser degree of every elector.

I spoke earlier of my friend who believed in democracy but not in defending it by force. We may be driven to be pacifists and to disavow once and for all and absolutely the force upon which it rests; but then we should be quite honest about what our 'belief' in democracy amounts to. For by doing this we have deliberately upset the incredibly complicated equilibrium of power upon which depends the achievement of any social justice for which hitherto we have been fighting. In fact, it is not upset —but only because there are not enough pacifists.

The dilemma is a terribly poignant one. If you say that under no circumstances you will ever be party to the decisive weapon of power, then you are really washing your hands in advance of any final responsibility for the structure of justice. You are saying in effect, 'This power is now so evil, it is of the devil; it is no longer of God. I cannot accept responsibility for it in order to see that, like other power, it is *used*, used to express love through justice. I can only renounce it, and therewith abandon the whole equilibrium out of which alone some justice can come.' Unless one is prepared to work *within* the power equilibrium and therefore accept, if only to negotiate the limitation of, the ultimate sanction, one is deliberately throwing away the current coin through which alone love is able to do any business in the world of systems. This means ultimately confining love of one's neighbour to the realm of pure personal relationship—a limitation against which the whole Prophetic tradition stands in protest. It is abandoning all the 'orders' of social life—from the family at one end to international power politics at the other—simply to what St Paul calls 'wrath'.

The Christian must always hold to the fact that the imperative of love may indeed at any time demand such action of him: he must be prepared to 'hate' all these for Christ's sake and the Gospel's. It may involve him in the absolute renunciation of power—and therefore necessarily, in some form, in death. For let us not blink at this. Power is nothing but the sum total of all those vitalities by which organized social life is maintained. There is an essential and indefeasible connection between what is expressed in the two Greek words *bia*, force, and *bios*, life. No life is possible without power. This gets focused very clearly in time of war. As long as a man holds a ration-book, he cannot escape involvement in the power situation. Even the most active dissociation of himself from it does not enable him to contract out of it. As Middleton Murry graphically put it, out of every £1 made from the sale of *Peace News* during the last war, 10s went to financing armaments. And if that was true of the last war it will be even more true of the next—as indeed it is already true of our present situation. In fact, I sometimes wonder whether the whole distinction between being a pacifist and being a non-pacifist is any longer a meaningful one. Of course, it makes a difference, at present, to whether a young man consents to do national service—or, rather, in what form he elects to do it; and it affects the kind of projects, within narrow limits, upon which a few atomic physicists are prepared to work. But what real difference is there between the physicist who finally perfects the H-bomb, or the service-man who presses the last button, and the rest of us, except that we are free to make varyingly agonized noises of disapproval? We are all involved: renunciation of any element in the power situation can only be symbolic as long as we remain in it by staying alive. The witness of the celibate, the ascetic, the pacifist, is always of this relative, parasitic character: it is one that could not be universalized without life in this world becoming impossible. The pacifist lives on the power, as the celibate lives on the paternity, against which he witnesses.

Furthermore, and of greater practical significance, is the fact that this kind of witness, precisely because it renounces the power complex, can never be enforced upon others. This makes it problematic how far pacifism can ever be translated into a legislative programme. The dilemma can be seen very clearly in the case of a man who preaches renunciation of the world in another form, namely, the ascetic. Whatever poverty he may be prepared to accept for himself, it is questionable whether he has any right to advocate it as part of an economic programme which must bring these consequences on millions of his fellow citizens, whether they like it or not. The ascetic must love his neighbour in the mass by voting for the welfare state: he cannot force poverty on others as law. And is not the pacifist equally committed, whatever his personal witness, to love his neighbour within the world of systems by maintaining that power structure by which the most adequate justice and respect for personality can be preserved—even when this structure depends ultimately on the threat of the bomb? Can he love his neighbour by compelling his martyrdom? When Jesus went to his death he took precautions that his disciples should *not* be implicated in it. The way of the Cross was indeed his will for them: but it must be chosen *by* them, in their own time.

But, from the other side, *can* a man ever love his neighbour by being party to dropping the bomb on him? If you are prepared to enter any structure which depends ultimately on the *threat* of the bomb (and the whole of our contemporary civilization does), then the implication is that you are prepared to use it—and God knows if I am.

I see no easy answer to this dilemma. And it is precisely because pacifists seem to me to imply that there is, if not an easy, at any rate a simple answer, that I never find at the last turn that I can go with them. The implication of the Quaker position, as I under-stand it, that all Christians, *if they were really Christian*, would be pacifists, I find tremendously compelling, but just too simple; and when it is immediately translated into political judgements it is often frankly exasperating, because it rides roughshod over political realities which any responsible statesman—and therefore any responsible voter—is bound to take into account.

I should be the last to deny the place of the pacifist—or of the monk. From the religious side there is, as I see it, an imperative need for the absolute witness to be made (relative and com-promised as this must be if one remains alive to make it), pointing always to the way of the Cross and to the ultimate Christian definition of power in terms of Christ crucified. But the logic of this witness is death—which includes dying to politics, to political action, political responsibility and political power. If pacifists can in practice have it both ways, it is because there are not enough of them—and because other *Christians* are providing a framework within which their witness is politically tolerated and indeed politically influential. That there never should be these other Christians is not a position that I personally could accept.

And yet, once more, can a *Christian* have the bomb in his locker? Involvement in the power structure drives one constantly further and further along the road, from the bow and arrow to the H-bomb. In this situation I can utterly understand the position of a man like Martin Niemöller, who was not previously a pacifist, but who now feels things have reached the point where

*anything* must be better than letting off this. And yet, if all
Christians contract out of the one operative policy which shows
any likelihood of containing this thing by agreement, is the
desired result any nearer? Are we to say that a Christian cannot
take his place at the disarmament table? Presumably not. Yet a
place at that table presupposes that you go in with your cards, not
without them. And, however magnificent it may sound as a
gesture, you do not really influence the course of the game by
discarding your aces before you start: you merely retire from it—
especially in a game where one party would gladly agree to play
without aces, since it holds all the kings! And is to remain in the
game, to hold your aces, as evil as using them? Even if a policy
resting on the threat of the bomb logically implies not merely
the power but in the last resort the will to use it, may there not
still be a real moral distinction between using it and not using
it—yet? We had the will, if necessary, and not merely the power
to use poison gas in the last war, but we did not. Are we in
morally the same position as if we had?

I have argued the case for the non-pacifist, for the Christian's
participation in the power struggle, as strongly as I can, because
I think it is increasingly becoming the more difficult case to
sustain. I still accept it; I am still not persuaded by the pacifist.
But I am in much greater danger, if that is the right word (and
I suspect that is how most Americans would see it!), of being
persuaded by events. For the situation is rapidly changing. There
has, for instance, in recent months[1] been a new phenomenon on
the British scene. The Campaign for Nuclear Disarmament,
which has been written off in America (as well as by much of the
English press) as pacifist, leftist, Labourite, Communist (or whatever the current or the local slur word may be), represents, I
believe, a much more profound reappraisal than anything I detect
going on in public thinking over here in the States. I am sure
such a reappraisal will also be forced upon you. But under the
smart of the *sputnik* I fear it will take a long time. For the effect
of this last has been to retrench all the most conventional

[1] I have not attempted to bring the political references up to date, as the
scene moves so swiftly.

and monolithic attitudes to power. It has been the signal to 'press on with the program', without turning aside to listen to any new or dangerous thinking that might have the effect of undermining it—and indeed would have the effect of undermining it.

For I believe that a quite radical revaluation of the realities of power is being pressed upon us. This, I would stress, is not the result of any pacifist or 'soft' thinking about power (not that these two are necessarily to be equated). It is the result of some very hard headed and realistic thinking. It stems from the growing recognition that the ultimate power is turning out to be no power, because it is a power we cannot use. If Aesop had lived today, he might have written a fable about the bee, who one day became conscious of the fact that he could not use his sting except in the act of dying. The agonizing reappraisal of power relationships within the animal kingdom resulting from this sobering discovery would make a pleasing study. But something no less radical is likely within our generation to be forced upon the thinking of the human family. If not, it will surely perish; for the bee at least destroys only himself in his final act of power. But it is not merely, as we in England have come to recognize and you, with the perfection of the Intercontinental Ballistic Missile, must surely see, that the final sanction can be used only to commit suicide. It is that, short of this point, almost all previous power strategy is becoming out-dated. We are like the dinosaur, weighed down with an armament we cannot use. We sit in Cyprus with planes stacked with H-bombs, yet the Russians control Syria under our very noses. Power, when it is not the sort you can use, becomes merely an embarrassment and a weakness.

One of the few who have had the courage to push through what he calls 'the thought-barrier' at this point is Sir Stephen King-Hall, well known in England as a former naval commander and Member of Parliament and as editor for the past twenty years of one of the most informed and intelligent political news-letters. He is certainly not 'soft' in his thinking; but in his book, *Defence in the Nuclear Age*, he coolly argues, against a background of service experience, for unilateral nuclear disarmament; and he is prepared to think through the consequences of this into realms where most of our minds simply boggle. I am not saying he is wholly right. But I cite the book as a response, and a very creative and courageous one, to what I do believe is a new situation. For King-Hall is no pacifist: he is arguing about defence, about how to make *war*. He comes to the conclusion he does by going right into the power situation, not by contracting out. It may not be magnificent—his programme for passive resistance even under occupation offers singularly little *éclat*—but at least it is politics. To be sure, it is not immediately practical politics (though disturbance at the present Government's nuclear policy—which is American nuclear policy—probably swung at least one British by-election[1]); but it has defined the issue in political terms. And for me at any rate it has *begun* to resolve the almost unbearable dilemma posed by the either-or of accepting the nuclear rat-race or condemning oneself to political sterilization.

But this still leaves virtually untouched the problems introduced by the specifically *Christian* understanding of power. God's self-definition of power is terrifyingly simple—as simple and as terrifying as the Cross. He has exposed the strong right arm by which he wills to curb the nations, and it is pierced with nails, stained with blood and riveted in impotence. That is still an almost insurmountable offence to our political thinking. In consequence, we either transfer our worldly conceptions of power into our Christian moral judgements or we try to resolve the complexities of the political situation by texts from the Sermon on the Mount. The great man, the true prophet, is the man who can see the moral issue as simple as it is—as simple as Jesus always saw it—and the political issue as complex as it is. I have, I fear, merely succeeded in muddying the moral issue by the political. But let me end with two quotations, one from a man who possesses the simplicity of true greatness, the other from one who in my experience is seldom lucid, but whose compassion with the pathos of our age enables him often to reach down to that fundamental simplicity where deep speaks to deep. These two

[1] And has since had perceptible repercussions on the policy of the Labour Party.

men are in fact both pacifists, and indeed my very respect for them on this issue is part of my own racked condition.

The first is Dr C. H. Dodd. 'It may', he writes (and it is a recognition that I do not find in most pacifists), 'be neither possible nor desirable for nations to act like the man who turns the other cheek; but even at such a moment like this in the affairs of the world, human action is wrong unless it partakes of *this quality*, of patient and unself-seeking respect for the other party, however objectionable; and aims in *this direction*, towards overcoming evil with good. Unless it does so, it is not only wrong, but ultimately disastrous.'[1] In other words, we must never allow the specifically Christian definition of power to be regarded as relevant merely in the realm of personal relationships, but not in the world of systems; merely at the level of grace, but not at that of nature; merely in the Church, but not in the world. To retreat into that solution of the problem—and in practice it is the first and easiest retreat that is open—is the final abdication. For it denies that *all* the power, like all the wisdom, of God is to be understood in terms of Christ and him crucified. It says that the Cross is all very well in the sanctuary, but that we must look to some more workable definition of power for the 'summit'. And that ultimately is to believe in two gods.

The other quotation is from Professor D. M. Mackinnon. 'Should the issue of atomic war be presented', he said once in a broadcast,[2] 'the Christian may well hesitate and ask himself whether acceptance of such a struggle will not altogether jeopardize the possibility of charity. If rule of law is, as to the Western mind it often appears, a true middle term between force and love, coercion and pity, are the essentially lawless methods of modern war the way to vindicate that rule? Yet if we say "No" to those methods, what is left for us in such circumstances which we may call political action—action directed, that is, to sustain and defend the ordered fabric of human existence? To this problem it seems Christians have at present no real answer—a terrible comment on the extent to which they have allowed their politics to fall apart

[1] *Gospel and Law*, p. 81.
[2] Reprinted in *Two Worlds in Focus* (National Peace Council), p. 43.

from the vivifying influence of their prayer, their prayer from a true concern for men where they are.'

It *is* a terrible comment. And yet it is within the Church, the body of the Word made flesh that the resources are to be found, if they are to be found anywhere, for breaking down this dichotomy. How at any rate we may begin to unite politics and prayer, and prayer with a concern for 'men where they are', will be my theme in the third and last lecture.


## 3. LITURGY

IN THE TWO PREVIOUS lectures, I started from the doctrine of creation. For it is constantly necessary to stress that matter and power belong to God, and that therefore the first, and the last, thing that the Christian has to say to them is 'Yes'. But in between he has to say a good many more equivocal things. For both matter and power give organized expression also to all that is most corrupting, depersonalizing and diabolic in the world we know.

But in this last lecture I am not so much concerned with what, as Christians, we *say* about them, but with what we *do* about them; or, rather, with how we may enter into what *God* is doing about them in this world as we know it between the first creation and the last. I do not propose here to go into the field of social and political action—though let us be clear that that is where the redemption of power and matter has to be worked out, and any sort of Christian witness which thinks it can avoid this implication stands condemned as not being concerned with the whole man. What I want to do is again to look to the fundamentals, and to explore the basic significance for all Christian action of *the* Christian action, the action which lies at the heart of the whole Church's life, the command given by Jesus to his disciples when he said to them, '*Do* this, in remembrance of me.'

This may seem a surprising sequel to the two previous lectures. But it is surprising only because the Holy Communion has in the minds of most of us become completely dissociated from the world of matter and power. It is connected with the sanctuary rather than the city, with the soul's relationship to God rather than with man's relationship to society. And yet basically it is about matter and society, bread and the sharing of bread. It is indeed concerned with the most sacred, yet at that very point with the most common: it is the *Holy Communion*. And the word 'liturgy' which for us has exclusive reference to what goes on in church had in origin a very different reference. It is a term derived from the realm of municipal affairs, of local politics. In ancient Greece a citizen might be called upon to discharge his responsibility to the community, such as we should pay in rates or income tax, by making himself responsible for some piece of public works, like repairing the local dockyard or equipping so many men for the militia. This was called his *leitourgia*; and the word is derived from *laos*, people, and *ergon*, work. From this it came, in due course, to be applied to *the* Christian social action, *the ergon* of the *Laos* or people of God.

I should like to consider with you some of the implications of this action. For the reason why the Christian doctrine of matter has become dissociated from its understanding of spirit, the reason why, in Professor Mackinnon's words, 'we have allowed our politics to fall apart from the vivifying influence of our prayer', is largely that we have let slip from the centre of our lives and thinking that very thing in our religion which inescapably unites spirit and matter, prayer and politics—namely, the sacraments. For it is here that the religion of the Word made flesh receives its crucial, continuing and most distinctive expression. This connection has been obscured by the fact that so many in our Churches who have been keenest on sacramental revival have desired it for reasons which are utterly irrelevant to this, and indeed have the effect of making religion *more* churchy, *more* sanctuary-minded, and *less* vitally concerned with 'men where they are'.

But let me try to draw out three points at which a truer understanding of what liturgy is about and a more complete earthing of our religion in the consecration of bread may in fact point the way through from prayer to politics, from the holy to the common, from the world of spirit to the world of matter.

(1) The first thing I would wish to emphasize is that at this point we have the pattern and the power-house of all Christian *action*. We are only too familiar within Christian history with the endemic divorce between faith and life, belief and action, worship and work. Yet at the very heart of our Faith and at the very heart of our worship has all along been something which is itself inescapably *action*, as the command, 'Do this', and the regular expression of the early Church, 'doing the Eucharist', remind us. We cannot be involved in this without being involved in action, for it is of its very nature. Nor is it just *an* action, which this particular form of public worship happens to involve. It is, rightly understood, *the* Christian action, from which all other Christian action flows. This is because it is not in the first place an action of ours at all, but an action of Christ's. Nor, again, is it just *an* action of Christ's; it is *the* saving act of Christ, as it is here and now made present and operative. 'When you reflect after Communion, said P. T. Forsyth, ' "What have I done to-day?" say to yourself, "I have done more than on any busiest day of the week. I have yielded myself to take part with the Church in Christ's finished Act of Redemption, which is greater than the making of the world".' When we come to Communion it is to the very drama of our redemption that we come, in the literal and original sense of that word *drama*, 'the thing done'. We come not simply to a miming of it, as to a passion play, but to the thing done itself, or rather to the doing of it. For we come here to the Cross, to the Lord's death. And here too we come to the Consummation: we enter that new world to which already by Baptism we belong. For at this point both the past and the future converge upon the present. Calvary in all its power comes to us: the very body and blood of Christ himself, once broken and given *for* us, is here broken and given *to* us. We do not have to strain to see how an atonement made two thousand years ago can still be relevant; for here it is in all its potency, streaming into our sinful present, restoring and recreating our lives. And here too 'we taste

the powers of the age to come'. Week by week, in the Spirit (that 'element of the end within the present'), on the Lord's day (itself the pledge of that 'day of the Lord' when the rule of this world shall finally have passed to God and his Christ), the baptized come together to be built up into the body of Christ, into that part of the new, resurrection order already at work within the structures of the old.

All this is included in the *anamnesis* of himself which Christ commanded us to make, and to which he attached the promise of his presence. It has been no small factor in the weakness and disunity of western Christendom that there has been no other word available for this than 'memorial', or the 'perpetual memory' of Cranmer's consecration prayer. For there could be no more dismal misunderstanding of the Eucharist than to think of it as a mere memorial service, in which we remind ourselves of someone no longer with us. On the contrary, this is what brings the past *out* of the past—and the future *out* of the future—and makes them both operative in the here and now. The whole work of Christ *for* us is here made over *to* us in such a way that we actually participate in the blood, that is, the sacrificial death, and the body, that is, the resurrection life, of Christ. These become ours now, to redeem and transform our lives and the world we live in and to deal creatively with its evil and frustration.

And here is the basis for the whole of the Church's social action. If we are to be biblical in our thinking, we cannot find the foundation for our social action in the old Liberal slogan of 'building the kingdom of God'—for the New Testament no-where tells us to 'build' the kingdom of God. Nor can we rest in the much more insidious alternative of a view of the Kingdom which excuses us from social action altogether:

> Sit down, O men of God,
>   His kingdom he will bring,
> Whenever it shall please his will;
>   You cannot do a thing.

The ground for Christian social action is the action of *Christ* about his saving work—everything apart from that is mere 'good works', and the kingdom of God cannot be raised on our good works. The Kingdom is Christ, recreating the world, his world, now. And *our* action lies in entering into, participating in, that action. And the primary point at which he lays this participation upon us is in that act in which above all he is the doer, when he says to *us*, together, 'Do this'. No communicant can suppose that the Kingdom can come except in so far as Christ's action becomes ours. For *the* Christian action, that *par excellence* which mediates Christ's saving work to the world, is, always and essentially, the action of Christ *in his body*.

This is what the Church, as the body of Christ, exists to do for the world. This is our 'liturgy', the piece of public work laid upon us within this world as citizens of God's commonwealth. The Eucharist is the gospel of the Kingdom in action, the proclaiming of the Lord's death till he comes; it is the manifesto, not only in word but in deed, of all Christ has done, is doing and will do to change the world—the notice of the new order served upon it.

Now if the Liturgy is all this, two things follow. The first is that we must let the action speak in such a way that those involved in it can be under no illusion that something tremendous *is* here being *done*, and that they, all of them, are the agents in it. But I suspect that most people have not the remotest notion after attending a typical Communion service that they have been taking part in a piece of social action. What is *done* has been so completely buried under what is said, and has in any case been almost wholly devolved upon one man, that this is scarcely surprising. But we *must* find a way, each according to our own tradition, of letting the action itself speak; we must allow the structure of it, 'the shape' of the Liturgy, to stand out, based as it is not upon a pattern of words or prayers, but upon Jesus' own fourfold action in the upper room, when he took, and blessed, and broke, and gave. And then we must find a way of giving everyone a really dynamic share in it, restoring to the different parts of the body of Christ those elements in the corporate action which are not properly the 'liturgy' of the presiding priest or minister at all, but which, with the increasing clericalization of the service, have become attached to him in Catholic and Protestant tradition alike.

The details of this belong to the sphere of liturgical reform—though such reform is usually so taken up with altering what is *said* that the much more important, and much less controversial, task is ignored, of bringing out what is *done*. Into details of ways and means I do not propose to enter now.[1] But I should like just to say why I have come to believe that these things matter so much.

When I was a theological student there was no subject that seemed to me more utterly remote from evangelism and the real work of the Kingdom than liturgiology. And, in the way it is commonly taught, I am still inclined to feel the same. But since I first found myself responsible for the life of a worshipping community, I have come to see it very differently. Liturgy, I am convinced, is a first priority in evangelism, in the whole showing forth of the Lord's death. For what is this but the very heart of the gospel in action? We are always speaking of this service as the centre of the Christian life. What men see, or fail to see, when they look to this centre should, on our own showing, tell them how *we* at any rate understand the heart of the gospel. But when I consider a typical celebration of the Holy Communion I should really be horrified for anyone to think that *that* was how I understood the gospel of the new world in action. Can we with confidence point men to this as the 'hot spot' of the new creation, as the place above all where they may see what happens when Christ comes transformingly into the structures of this world order? We *must* let the Liturgy speak what it is meant to be proclaiming, or our evangelism is discredited at its very heart. And if the action, the drama, of God's redemption is not seen for what it is in church, by those involved in it, then it certainly will not be outside.

[1] Simply as an illustration of one way in which this can be done I may perhaps be allowed to refer to what we tried to work out in my own College Chapel at Cambridge. Copies of the manual, *The Holy Communion*, which set this out, may be obtained from The Dean, Clare College, Cambridge, for 3/- post free. A fuller account of this and an extension of the themes of this essay will be found in my forthcoming book, *Liturgy Coming to Life*.

And that brings me to the other corollary of seeing liturgy as social action. The Liturgical Movement, which has brought a breath of new life into all our denominations, will be under terrible indictment if all it affects in the end is the way things are 'done' in church. That is the awful warning provided by the Oxford Movement, in some at any rate of its later forms. The great hope I see in more recent movements, such as *Parish and People* in the Church of England and the Iona Community in Scotland, is that they do contain within them the clue to the way through and out into corporate action by the worshipping community in the neighbourhood and the world. For, let us make no mistake, it is by this that the Liturgical Movement will be judged, by the world—and by God.

(2) If the first thing that liturgy means is *action*, the second thing that lies at the heart of it is *matter*. In its original secular sense liturgy was the social equivalent of the department of public works. And the Liturgy is the most materialistic thing to which the Church sets its hand. At its very centre are pieces of matter, bread and wine, and without them the action could not begin at all.

And notice too that the matter concerned is not raw materials but manufactures. The matter of the sacrament of Baptism is water, something wholly God-given, signifying that man here contributes nothing. But the physical basis of the Holy Communion is the raw material of God's creation *as we have worked upon it*. The Eucharist presupposes production, and all the means of production, distribution and exchange that lie behind every crumb of bread and drop of wine. No production, no communion. 'If a man will not work neither shall he eat' is the law of the spiritual life also.

This emphasis is important in connection with the Christian doctrine of matter, and is what distinguishes it from pagan religion and from much harvest-festival religion. When men are not altogether averse to any connection between matter and religion, they lean to the idea that God can be encountered in 'nature'—that is, in unspoilt nature. 'God made the countryside, man made the town' is a theme that evokes a ready response in all of us. Bread and wine seem to take us further from God than earth and water, not nearer to him; the element of production bars more than it mediates the divine encounter. At our harvest festivals we fill our churches with vegetable marrows, to the exclusion of the much more questionable manufactures, which bear the smear of trade and industry. In this way we seek to find a way to God through matter that by-passes the need for redemption.

But the Eucharist by insisting that the point of contact between God and man in Christ is not raw material, nothing wild or 'unspoilt', not even the cultivated wheat and vine, but bread and wine, refuses to let us evade the real crux. This can be stated as follows: On the one hand, God the eternal Worker creates man to be a worker: the purpose of creation and the destiny of man are fulfilled when they meet in the fruit of their co-operation. Only *homo faber* can fully meet and communicate with the creator God. And yet, on the other hand, *homo faber*, industrial man, so far from alone being able truly to shape the worth of his Maker, is in fact the most completely insulated against the touch of the Eternal. The world is indeed 'charged with the grandeur of God', as Gerard Manley Hopkins wrote; but

> Generations have trod, have trod, have trod;
>   And all is seared with trade; bleared, smeared with toil;
>   And wears man's smudge and shares man's smell: the soil
> Is bare now, nor can foot feel, being shod.

The Eucharist by requiring manufactures for its elements refuses to burke this reality. For bread stands not simply for the bounty of God and the wholesome work of man; it stands for all those things that have made it also the symbol of our penury—the exploitation of man and nature, the bitterness of competition and class conflict, all the organized selfishness of tariffs and price-rings, a world distribution that brings plenty to some but malnutrition to millions more. And the wine, the bottle, is the symbol not simply of freedom and joy, of holiday and wedding feast, but also of some of life's most tragic forms of degradation—drunkenness and broken homes, and all the wretched sordidness of sensuality and debt.

But it was precisely these things—the bread and the wine that

c

wore man's smudge and shared man's smell—that Jesus took; and in the action of the Eucharist he takes them still. And over them he says the astonishing words, '*This* is *my* body . . . *This* is *my* blood'. He identifies himself with them, and claims them for that order of life to which he himself belongs. Only thus can they be restored to what they were created to be—the means of contact between God and man.

Outside the Eucharistic relation the division between the holy and the common, the sacred and the secular, remains; but within it is abolished. The bread and wine, secularized by human sin, are taken by Christ, with all they represent of human life, and over them are spoken the words of consecration. But our lives can be made one with his life, this world order remade as the kingdom of God, only through the Cross. Our bread must be broken in his hands, our lives poured out in sacrifice with his, if they are to become the carriers of his risen power. And so he takes, he blesses—and *breaks*. And then he gives. He gives himself; he gives us of his new creation, this foretaste of all matter redeemed to its true and proper relation; and he gives us back our own lives restored now as members of his body, all the corrupted and sinful relationships of this world knit up into that holy community which is the pledge and the instrument of all creation's destiny.

The pledge and the instrument—for what is here done to this material order by the hand of Christ must through us be made true of every area of life. The bread and the wine over which he says, 'This is my body, my blood', are samples only—taken by Jesus off the supper table 'as they were eating'. This relationship is one into which the whole material and social order must be brought if it is to be redeemed. And this again has two implications.

The first essential is that the way we do things in church should make it clear that we ourselves do believe this, namely, that there is for us no division between the bread and wine we use in this service and all other bread and wine and all other matter. But the typical Anglican celebration, to go no further than our own tradition, contrives to make this connection about as obscure as it could be—wafers in place of ordinary bread, or bread pressed and diced into some unrecognizable form, wine supplied by ecclesiastical purveyors that no one in their senses would ever drink for pleasure, served up in ecclesiastical cruets by altar-boys in fancy dress. The whole thing reeks of a conception of holiness that is almost the complete opposite of everything for which Christianity stands, a conception of the holy defined in purely Jewish terms, as that which is *not* common. For our own College Communion at Cambridge we insisted upon an ordinary loaf baked in the College kitchens and some claret from the College cellars brought up in a good secular decanter by a couple of ordinary undergraduates. Unless the bread and wine we offer at Communion really comes off the table of our common lives, out of the midst of our weekday world, then there is nothing for the process of redemption to work on; it is not our real lives that we are asking God to deal with. And I am coming more and more to believe that this false sense of holiness is so pervasive and such a barrier that for a great many people the veil is not going to be removed until they see the whole thing taken out of a consecrated building altogether—from the sanctuary to the kitchen table. The movement towards the recovery of the Church in the house, and the breaking of bread at this level, would seem to me of quite prime significance. For somehow we must get through to people, in such a way that they can really see it—which means usually in such a way that they can literally see it—that this is a *meal* before it is a 'service'. For otherwise they will never see its connection with any other meal. And if they do not see its connection with any other meal, they are unlikely to see it with any other matter. And if they do not see it with any other matter, indeed with all other matter, then what we are doing in church is not properly speaking liturgical action at all: it is theatre—and when we come out of the theatre we step into an entirely disconnected world.

And this leads to the second corollary, that we make this connection equally real *out* of church. Just as I found that people were shocked that we insisted on bringing secular things into chapel, so at first they were even more shocked when we deliberately took out the remainder of the loaf, which we had offered but not consecrated, to be shared round and actually eaten with butter and marmalade at breakfast. So divorced have become our eating habits in church and out of it! But such a breakfast, though it restores the integral connection of the Communion with a common meal, is after all but the symbol for something much more far-reaching. 'When we come together to break bread', said a seventeenth-century writer, 'we must break it to the hungry, to God himself in his poor members'. The sharing of bread, concluded sacramentally, has to be continued socially—and thence economically and politically. And the economic consequences of the Eucharist—of sharing bread—are potentially very dangerous in a country like yours or mine that enjoys a standard of living which is that of Dives to most of the rest of the world.

Are we not all of us ready to accept outside Communion what at Communion we would not tolerate? We set up a double standard. Let me illustrate this from a particularly prickly area of life over here. When I was on my first visit to the States, and very innocent, I was taken to be shown a beautiful eighteenth-century church in the oldest part of one of your southern cities. As happens, this church now found itself in what had gradually deteriorated into a completely negro quarter. But not a single negro worshipped in it, or could. This did not very easily square with the story I had been told that segregation in church was of course only natural since coloureds and whites resided in separate areas. But there *was* one negro in the church, the old verger, for whom this was his life. 'But naturally', I said, 'he will communicate here?' 'Oh, no', was my host's reply, 'he couldn't do that!' That was to me, and still is, a terrible contradiction of the gospel. And yet, as I thought about it afterwards, I wondered if it was *more* terrible than the contradiction that would have been set up had they been prepared to share bread here but declined, as social custom dictated, to share it outside, at home or in restaurants? But do we really believe that what we do outside Communion, in attitude to people or to matter, *is* of such consequence as what we do at Communion? This is just what the Corinthians could not see—that their refusal to share their purely secular sandwiches before Communion meant it was impossible for them to eat the Lord's Supper. For what they would then eat, what they would be invoking upon themselves in judgement, was the very thing their conduct denied, namely, the body of Christ, the one new man. Have we anything like such an integrated understanding of Eucharist and society, liturgy and life? If we knew what we do when we come together to one place to break this bread!

(3) Thirdly, and briefly because I have already touched upon it, there lies at the very heart of the Liturgy not only Action and Matter, but Society. Liturgy is by its very nature social action: it is the *ergon* of the *laos*.

I am sure in these circles I hardly need to lay stress upon the corporate character of the Holy Communion, though I have found it the first point that one still has to insist upon year in and year out with every new batch of freshmen. The dye of pure individualism, Catholic and Protestant, is something that it will take generations to get out of our Confirmation preparation, our Communion teaching, our Communion manuals, and above all, our Communion practice. For, once more, it is how the action is *done* and *seen* to be done that in the end is more decisive than anything said from the pulpit or provided in the pew. Is this service seen inescapably to be the action, the concelebration, of the *whole* people of God?

Again, I will not go here into details of how this can be made effective in practice. I believe they are of the greatest importance; but they vary so much with our own traditions and with what is 'politically' possible in any local congregation.

Let me simply stress what I conceive to be the *essential* connection between liturgy and society. The corporate character of the Eucharist does not consist simply in the fact that we all do this together and must necessarily do it together. The teaching of the New Testament is not that we can do together what I cannot, but 'because of the one loaf, we who are many are one body' (I Cor. 10.17). The unity is not something from which we can presume to start, except in so far as 'in Christ' we are always and only becoming what we are. The corporeity is something created, or rather recreated, by our participation in the one loaf. By ourselves, even as a group, we are many, fragmented: it is the unity which Christ makes of us, the unity of the one new man, that alone gives us the theological right to say 'we'. As St Chrysostom put it, 'We become one single body, limbs of his flesh and bone. This is the effect of the nourishment he gives us; he merges himself in us in order that we may all be one single thing, as one body, joined to one head'. It is the Pauline mystery, so powerfully expounded by St Augustine, of the double sense of 'the body'— that we *are* the body of Christ as we feed on the body of Christ— which is the specifically Christian clue to the renewal of society. With this goes the corollary that we cannot receive his body in the sacrament except as we are knit up into his body the Church: we cannot have Christ without his members. And the implications of that—that there *is* no Communion without community —are of unlimited consequence once we begin to take them seriously.

The effect of Holy Communion, week by week, year by year, is, as it were by a process of continuous creation, constantly to be propagating holy community, though creating it not *ex nihilo* but out of the existing material of ordinary sinful human lives and human relationships—out of the 'we who are many'. Or, rather, that is what it should be doing. And again, if the Gospel is to have any power, and if we ourselves are not to be condemned with the world, we must see that it does.

First of all must this be done within the action of the service itself—and the expression of it in church will be of greater rather than less importance to us the more concerned we are for the social implications of the gospel. Does the way we meet to celebrate leave upon people, whatever else they may miss, an inescapable sense of having been involved in the renewing of a fellowship of supernatural quality and power? Is everything we do in church, from where we sit onwards, subjected to the Pauline test of all liturgical activity? Does it, that is to say, produce *oikodomia*?—which does not mean in modern English 'Is it edifying?' but 'Is it constructive of community?'

And then, secondly, does this visible and tangible sense of community within the Liturgy really express itself in the life of the congregation outside? That is a banal question, but until it is answered there is no use talking about the third stage, the impact of this fellowship upon the neighbourhood. And unless we do go on to this third stage, the body of Christ becomes a coterie. And that is the final condemnation of the Church, for then it shuts up the kingdom of heaven against men.

Just as this Eucharistic action is the pattern of all Christian action, the sharing of this Bread the sign for the sharing of all bread, so this Fellowship is the germ of all society renewed in Christ. It is part of the mystery of the kingdom of God (and indeed the ultimate ground of Christian hope) that we are not called upon to 'build' or 'bring in' something which does not yet exist, but to build up and bring out something already in our midst, the new order introduced into this world by the life, death and resurrection of Jesus and entered by every man when he 'puts on Christ'. It is this new world already operative within the old—the resurrection body of history, the body of Christ—to which the Christian exists to witness. The destiny which Christ holds out for matter, for power and for society, is comprehended in the single great purpose, already begun, of the conforming of the body of our humiliation—this entire structure of sorrow, sin and death—to the likeness of his glorious body. That is the Christian's goal, and his social task. And the point *par excellence* where the new creation breaks through into this, where the pattern and the power of the new world is given, and where the new community which is its instrument is fashioned, is the Holy Communion. Let us then never lose grip on its centrality, nor allow ourselves to reckon liturgy of little significance, if these great social concerns are at the heart of what we mean by the Gospel.

I am done. I have not answered the practical and most pressing questions from which I started. I have not tried to. All I have attempted is to point to the kind of biblical thinking about matter and power, and above all to the quality of Christian community, out of which I pray that these answers will be drawn by men wiser and more deeply involved than I in the power structures of this very material, God-given world.

# CHAPTER FOUR

# The Priesthood of the Church[1]

IN SPEAKING OF the priesthood of the Church it may sound paradoxical to begin by emphasizing how *little* ground there is for speaking of it. Yet surely one of the most remarkable facts in the history of religion is the astonishing and well-nigh total eclipse in the New Testament of the priestly side of the Old Testament religion. The great exception is, of course, the Epistle to the Hebrews. But while this Epistle affords a magnificent interpretation of the priesthood of Christ, it is virutally silent on the priestly aspect of the Church. As is well known, nowhere in the New Testament or in the early period of the Church is the word *hiereus*, priest, used of the Christian ministry, though all the other offices—bishop, presbyter and deacon—were evidently adapted from Jewish models.[2] The whole elaborate liturgy of the Temple and the sacrificial system which lay at the very centre of Jewish religion was given up with extraordinarily little heart-searching; the ritual requirement of circumcision was officially waived within twenty years; and the still more pervasive provision for ceremonial cleansing was abandoned almost at the drop of a hat. The *un*priestly character of early Christianity must surely have been one of the first things to strike an outsider, whether he were Jew or pagan. And we find Justin Martyr having in fact to defend the Faith precisely on this score.

It is instructive to contrast the early Christian Church at this

[1] An address to the Rochester Diocesan Clergy School, September 1957.

[2] I cannot resist quoting the striking anticipation of the episcopal ideal which occurs in 'The order for the superintendent of the camp' in the Damascus Document, xvi, of the Qumran Community: 'And he shall have mercy on them as a father on his sons, and shall bring back all their erring ones as a shepherd does with his flock. He shall loose all the ties that bind them, so that there shall be none oppressed and crushed in his congregation'.

point with the Qumran Community on the shores of the Dead Sea, with which so many other parallels have been drawn. There is indeed even here a superficial resemblance between them, for both found themselves at odds with official Sadducean priesthood and cut off from the Temple worship and its sacrifices. Moreover, the Qumran covenanters had a conception of spiritual sacrifice very like that which we find in the New Testament. But we should not be led into thinking that this was in any sense a 'lay' movement, rather like early Quakerism. On the contrary, they prided themselves on being the *true* Zadokites, and from their Manual of Discipline and the so-called Damascus Document we are left in no doubt that they were as priest-ridden as any section of Judaism. The leadership was overwhelmingly in priestly hands. In any group of ten or more there must be one priest. Their inner circle of twelve priests and three laymen contrasts strongly with the lay character of Jesus' chosen group. Again, in the Covenanters' hopes for the future, the priestly 'Messiah of Aaron' always takes precedence over the secular 'Messiah of Israel', whereas in the main body of Judaism the royal, Davidic hope is strongly to the forefront. If, as I believe to be a plausible hypo-thesis,[1] John the Baptist was brought up at Qumran, or at any rate had such a way of life as the background of his mission, we should not forget that he too was of priestly descent on both sides. And finally, the decisive difference between Qumran and Christianity lay in the centrality given by the former to con-stant acts of ablution and purification: the judgement of Jesus that nothing from without can defile a man would not have met with much response on the shores of the Dead Sea.

But if this *un*priestly quality was the characteristic of early Christianity that would have struck the casual observer most forcibly, the casual observer would, not for the last time, have been superficial in his judgement. For the priestly element in Judaism had not disappeared without trace: it had been trans-muted. It is indeed the speed and the thoroughness of this trans-mutation that is the truly remarkable fact.

[1] See my article 'The Baptism of John and the Qumran Community', *Harvard Theological Review*, L (1957), pp. 175-91.

In the first place, the early Church would have been unanimous that the priesthood, like the law and the prophets, had been fulfilled, not destroyed in Christ. (In fact, the priestly system was at least half of what the Jew meant by 'the Law'.) Jesus was the *true* high priest; he was the new Temple; in his atoning death the necessity for further sacrifices was exhausted; and the circumcision of Christ, in which the baptized shared, was the complete stripping off of the flesh-body of which the external rite had been but the partial symbol.

This aspect of the Christian fulfilment I need not dwell upon, since a lecture on the priesthood of Christ has preceded this. But it is quite the most important aspect, and all that I have to speak of is derivative from it. For the priesthood of the Church *is* nothing else than the priesthood of Christ flowing over into his body and exercised through his members. And precisely because it is Christ's priesthood, we must preserve a high doctrine of the priesthood of the Church, and never allow our fear of priesthood as we see it sometimes on earth to minimize the inescapably priestly character and calling that attaches to his whole body and to every member of it.

The obvious point from which to start is the application to the Church by two New Testament writers, the authors of I Peter and the Apocalypse, of two great Old Testament texts—Ex. 19.6, 'You shall be to me a kingdom of priests and a holy nation', and Isa. 61.6, 'You shall be called the priests of the Lord, men shall speak of you as the ministers of our God'.

It is very significant that, of the hundreds of Old Testament references to the priesthood, it should be these two alone which are applied to the Church. For here, almost uniquely in the Old Testament, it is the whole people of Israel who are designated priests, and not, as usually, one tribe or family succession within Israel. In a situation such as ours where the vocation to the ordained ministry is essentially a personal and spiritual calling, we can hardly appreciate the position which prevailed in Judaism, where to be a priest one had to belong to a certain line, and then all one had to do was to prove it. This idea of a closed hereditary priesthood is again one of the things that the Christian revolution abolished so summarily that we are scarcely aware from the New Testament that anything has happened at all.

The theme, to be found in these isolated passages of the Old Testament, that the whole of Israel was a priesthood was in practice obscured by the much more obvious fact that there was one tribe in Israel which was priestly and eleven that were not. But in the New Testament the theme comes to its own. 'You are a chosen race', says St Peter, perhaps to the newly baptized, 'a royal priesthood, a holy nation, God's own people' (I Pet. 2.9). 'Come then to him, to that living stone, rejected by men but in God's sight chosen and precious; and like living stones be your-selves built up into a spiritual house, to be a holy priesthood, to offer spiritual sacrifices acceptable to God through Jesus Christ' (I Pet. 2.4f.). And the seer of the Revelation strikes the same reson-ant chords in his doxology of 1.5f.: 'To him who loves us and has freed us from our sins by his blood and made us a kingdom, priests to his God and Father, to him be glory and dominion for ever and ever. Amen'; and again in his 'new song' of 5.9f.: 'Worthy art thou to take the scroll and to open its seals, for thou wast slain and by thy blood didst ransom men for God from every tribe and tongue and people and nation, and hast made them a kingdom and priests to our God, and they shall reign on earth' (cf. also 20.6).

These magnificent words speak for themselves, but I would have you notice one thing. The Reformers very rightly sought to restore this biblical emphasis in their doctrine of 'the priesthood of all believers'. But in practice this was often taken to mean 'the priesthood of *each* believer', just as Luther's profoundly biblical teaching on the freedom of a Christian man was perverted to imply that every man was his own pope. But the New Testament form of expression makes it quite clear that the priesthood and the royalty—the double authority, that is, of the Lord's Anointed, the Christ—is vested in the people of God *as a body*. It is held only *in solidum*. 'The Spirit', said F. D. Maurice once in a paradoxical remark, 'in an individual is a fearful contradiction'.[1] And the

---

[1] J. E. Maurice, *Life of F. D. Maurice*, I, p. 209, quoted by T. O. Wedel, *The Coming Great Church*, p. 78.

same applies to the priesthood. Indeed, there is an essential connection between the solidarity of the priesthood and the solidarity of the Spirit in the life of the Church. For one of the truly revolutionary claims and characteristics of the early Church was what it called 'the common ownership', the *koinonia*, of Holy Spirit. Hitherto the 'holy' had been defined as that which was *not* 'common'—and 'the holy' was the sphere of the priest. With the communalization of the holy went the communalization of the priesthood.

To the implications of this I shall return later. Let me round off the New Testament picture by referring you to what it says of the *function* of the Church in its priestly character. The people of God, says St Peter, has been called to be a holy and a royal priesthood for two tasks. The first is to 'offer spiritual sacrifices acceptable to God through Jesus Christ' (I Pet. 2.5); the second is to 'declare the wonderful deeds of him who called you out of darkness into his marvellous light' (2.9). In other words, it is called to the priesthood of Christ to act as the worshipping and as the witnessing community. Let me say a word on each.

It is in the worship of the Christian community that the priestly side of the Jewish religion finds its most obvious fulfilment, and it is here that the priestly language, of sacrifice, incense, altar, and liturgy, comes to its own in the New Testament. But again it is the transformation of all these that is surely the most striking. 'Through him then', concludes the writer to the Hebrews after his monumental demonstration of Christ as the great High Priest, 'let us continually offer up a sacrifice of praise to God, that is, the fruit of lips that acknowledge his name. Do not neglect to do good and to share what you have, for such sacrifices are pleasing to God' (13.15f.). This complete spiritualizing and ethicizing of the Christian sacrifice, even in a writer to whom ritual for its own sake evidently meant so much, is I think very remarkable. And it is borne out both by the seer of the Revelation, who, unlike most apocalyptists, was a liturgist in his bones, and by St Paul. 'The bowls of incense' *are* 'the prayers of the saints' (Rev. 5.8; cf. 8.3f.); and in Phil. 4.18 the 'fragrant offering, a sacrifice acceptable and pleasing to God' is the generosity of the

Philippians in supplying Paul's needs. For some reason this short epistle contains two more of Paul's very rare sacrificial metaphors (for he was a man evidently more at home in the law-court than the sanctuary). In 2.17 he speaks to the Philippians of the possibility of himself being 'poured as a libation upon the sacrificial offering of your faith' and in 2.30 of Epaphroditus 'risking his life to complete your service to me', where the word he uses is the same one, *leitourgia*, which in the previous passage was translated 'the sacrificial offering'. The use of this word *leitourgia* (liturgy), which, like *diakonia* (deaconing), is applied also to such an economic project as the collection for the Jerusalem churches (II Cor. 9.12), shows how completely in early Christianity liturgy was integrated with life. And this integration receives its classic expression in the words of Rom. 12.1: 'I appeal to you therefore, brethren, by the mercies of God, to present your bodies (your *somata*, your whole selves) as a living sacrifice, holy and acceptable to God, which *is* your spiritual worship'.

This same word, *leitourgia*, is used also to make the second connection, between worship and witness. Just as in II Cor. 3 and 4 St Paul can lead straight from the *diakonia* of Old Testament worship into the 'divine service' of Christian evangelism, so in Rom. 15.16 he speaks of his calling as 'a minister (*leitourgon*) of Christ Jesus to the Gentiles in the priestly service (*hierourgounta*) of the gospel of God, so that the offering of the Gentiles may be acceptable, sanctified by the Holy Spirit'. Do we as naturally think of our evangelism in terms of our priesthood, or of our priesthood in terms of our evangelism? For the priestly calling of the Church is to be defined just as much in terms of its witness as of its worship.

Now all that applies to *leitourgia* in general finds its focus supremely in *the* Liturgy, where work meets worship and worship issues in witness. And yet we have to recognize it as part again of the *un*priestly flavour of the New Testament writings that directly priestly language is not in fact applied by them to the Eucharist. We find Justin Martyr, in his defence of Christianity on this score, insisting that the Christians *do* have a sacrifice and that it finds its focus in the Eucharist. St Paul, moreover, in

I Cor. 10, plainly sees the Christian Eucharist as the equivalent of both Jewish and pagan sacrifices, in so far as each implies a communion in the altar or table of the deity. And the very use of the term 'the blood' of Christ, in this context, stamped as it had been with an atoning significance by Jesus at the last supper (Mark 14.24), carries inevitable sacrificial overtones. But nowhere in the New Testament is the Eucharist called a *thusia* or sacrifice, nor is its meaning drawn out in priestly categories.

This absence is the most remarkable in the Epistle to the Hebrews. Not once indeed in the Epistle is there a clear reference to the Eucharist, though the author certainly had a golden opportunity in the person of Melchizedek. He mentions everything else that is said about this figure in the Old Testament—and a good deal more—but fails to make any use of the statement, which the Fathers were not slow to seize upon, that this man, the priest of God Most High, 'brought forth bread and wine' (Gen. 14.18). Nowhere does he bring his doctrine of the sacrifice of Christ, or of his heavenly intercession, into relation with the Eucharist. The only possible exception is in 13.10, where he says, 'We have an altar from which those who serve the tent have no right to eat'. The context however makes it clear that the reference here is not to the Eucharist but to the Cross. The Cross is the Christian altar, outside the camp, at which the perfect sacrifice took place, once and for all. And even when the writer goes on, as he does immediately afterwards in 13.15, to speak of the sacrifice which must flow from *the* Christian sacrifice of the Cross, it is in terms not of the Eucharist but, as I said earlier, of the praise of the lips and the sharing of goods.

This, I think, can serve us as a salutary reminder. For there is no doubt that we shall relate the priestly task of the Church to the Liturgy—and we shall be entirely biblical in doing so,[1] since everything the Church does, and especially the heart of its worship, must be related to its priestly, as to its prophetic and pastoral, function. But while we shall certainly relate our priesthood to our liturgy, to 'services' *in* church, the danger is that we shall relate

---

[1] Cf., since this was written, A. Richardson, *An Introduction to the Theology of the New Testament*, ch. 16.

it effectively to little else. And that is where the New Testament, with its primary emphasis on service *of* the Church may be a useful corrective.

Let me now end by suggesting some points at which the New Testament teaching about the priesthood of the Church might with profit be brought to bear upon our own thinking and practice.

The general principle underlying all three is the one from which I started, namely, the change in the whole conception of the priesthood from the Old Testament to the New. In the Old Testament the priesthood, from a specified tribe, was to do *for* the people what the people as a whole could not do—in particular, to deal with their sins and restore their fellowship with God. In the New Testament the whole people of God is called to the priest-hood—the priesthood of Christ. It is called to share his priesthood to the world, mediating his atoning and reconciling work. In that priesthood every baptized member has a share. Within the Body there are, and were from the beginning, men ordained on its behalf to exercise, in the name of both its head and its members, the functions which belong to it as a whole. But this ordained ministry, which is priestly because the whole ministry of the Church is priestly, is in the strict sense representative, not vicari-ous. The priesthood does in the name of the Body what, essenti-ally, the whole Body is doing: it is not doing for the rest of its members what only it can do—except in so far as by ordination the Church as a whole deliberately reserves certain of its functions to certain authorized persons.

Let me then apply this principle to three points of our practice.

(1) The first is to *the* Liturgy of the Church.

The late Dom Gregory Dix in his article in the symposium, *The Parish Communion*, which he later expanded so superbly in *The Shape of the Liturgy*, traced the baleful development of the Eucharist from being in the early centuries the concelebration of the whole people of God, in which every order had its own function or 'liturgy', to something celebrated *by* the priest *for* the people. This development, which was scarcely affected by the Reformation, is something that has eaten very deep into our church consciousness. The Holy Communion has become the priest's service for which he is responsible and the laity are not—as one discovers very quickly if one takes a celebration in a village church where there is no priest. How are we to restore the idea that the 'celebrant' is not simply the priest—who in the early Church was called not the 'celebrant' but the 'president'—but rather the whole congregation of the people of God? That is, I believe, the first and indispensable step in enabling the laity to see their share in the priestly ministry of Christ's Church. But we clergy hardly help it by the set-up in which we are all too ready to acquiesce, let alone when we actively abet it by talking of celebrating *our* first communion or *my* mass.

(2) Secondly, I would instance our ministry of absolution. This is essentially part of the priestly function of the Church, and those can scarcely claim to be scriptural who would wish to minimize it. But again it is a ministry, of binding and loosing, retaining and remitting, which is vested in the Church corporately (Matt. 18.18; John 20.23). It is not vested in the priesthood as a group within the Church, though the *formal* exercise of it, in the name of the Church as a whole, may be authorized only to those ordained thereto. The latter qualification is understood well enough, the principle which it qualifies hardly at all. And how should our congregations understand it? For those who most would emphasize 'the priesthood of all believers' are those who speak of this ministry least, and *vice versa*.

But one of the main reasons, I am sure, why this ministry of absolution has been so stunted in our Church is because it has failed to be linked effectively with the doctrine of the priesthood of the whole Church. It has failed to be regarded as part of the normal function of the forgiving community. The Church is the community *par excellence* where forgiveness of sins is offered, where a man or a woman may be delivered from the isolation of sin into the renewing fellowship of the Holy Spirit. Sin is individual (though it is also depersonalizingly collective); forgiveness is corporate. That is why forgiveness can never simply be something between a man and his God, though that is where its heart lies. Forgiveness is essentially reconciliation, and for this the forgiving *community* is a *sine qua non*. If the absolution, whether in public or in private, is pronounced by the ordained priest, it is precisely because it is pronounced in the name of the whole Church, both catholic and local. As each member of the congregation listens to the absolution in church and says his 'Amen', he is just as much at the pronouncing end in relation to his fellow members as he is at the receiving end in relation to God. But again, how can we make that effective in practice as well as in principle—so that men may really see in the priesthood the reconciling fellowship, and in the reconciling fellowship not merely human friendship but the priesthood of Christ? I suspect this is one of the many points at which we may have to begin again, not at the level of the great Church and of the parish congregation, but in the 'cell' or 'house' Church. It is precisely the need for such a priestly ministry—and the lack of it—*right through the Church* down to its grass roots that has led to its substitute in Moral Rearmament.

(3) Thirdly, and finally, if this must be made true of the ministry of absolution, it has equally to be made true of the ministry of healing; or rather the need here is even greater, for the ministry of healing is not regarded as part of the regular ministry even of every ordained priest.

The two ministries of forgiveness and healing are, of course, inseparably connected, both in the needs of man and in the ministry of Jesus. It is all part of the priestly ministry of the Church, of its function to act as 'the salt of the earth', cleansing the life of this world from everything that stains and disfigures it. It is the task which Keats pictured so hauntingly of the sea, as he watched

> The moving waters at their priestlike task
> Of pure ablution round earth's human shores.

I will not say more of this ministry now than to stress again what is constantly obscured in its exercise, both within and even more outside the Church, that this is essentially and inescapably the function of the healing *community*. The work of healing is akin to the work of salvation: it is making men whole. And men cannot be made whole as individuals. They can be made whole only as their frayed and jarred lives are knit up into the seamless robe of Christ's body.

What I mean can be given in two illustrations. The first is from Mr T. S. Eliot's play, *The Cocktail Party*. That play is about the Church as the healing community, though the clinic takes the place of the confessional and 'the guardians' are a somewhat heavy disguise for the praying laity. But its theme is the priesthood of the Church in action, and, since we have so largely made it impossible for men to see this through the professional priest, it is good that they should be shown it in some other way.

The second illustration comes to me from a recent visit to the Iona Community. There, as part of the normal weekly worship of the Community, all visitors were invited to take their share— and I deliberately put it that way—in a service of healing. It was, I think, the most impressive I have attended. Nothing happened, no crutches were thrown away; indeed there were none to throw away. For, apart from the many absent sufferers prayed for by name, those of us there were a very ordinary cross-section of tied-up humanity. What was impressive was not simply that everyone was invited to come up and receive the healing, re-conciling power of Christ in his Church, but that any members of the congregation, men or women, who wished to were urged to come forward and to move round with the minister laying hands together in the name of the Church on those who desired it. Nothing was said, apart from simple words of Scripture. But one sensed there the priesthood of the Church being exercised very palpably, both in word and in deed. We went away knowing that we had seen and felt the healing community. How often do men see that in our churches?

# CHAPTER FIVE

# The House Church and the Parish Church[1]

'Paul . . . to the Church of God which is at Corinth' (*1 Cor. 1f.*)
'Paul . . . to the Church in your house' (*Philem. 1f.*)

THE CHURCH FOR THE New Testament is always the great Church, the *ecclesia* of God, the body of Christ. The biblical writers start there: they do not define the Church as Congregationalism does (and as Article XIX of the Church of England does when it begins: '*The* visible Church of Christ is *a* congregation of faithful men') in terms of the local unit, and then think of the universal Church as a federation of these units. But, while the Church is always the great Church, it can nevertheless, and must, be embodied in units which can still be described as 'the Church' —the Church as it finds expression 'at Corinth', 'in your house'. These units are not simply bits of the Church; they are the body of Christ in its totality, as it exists in this or that of its cells. Each cell is a microcosm, on its own scale perfectly reproducing the whole. This is an immensely important point for the doctrine of the local Church, and it is the truth which Congregationalism and our own Articles have so magnificently grasped—even though it is the wrong place from which to start a definition.

What I want to consider is the relation which should obtain between two levels of this Church-existence, between the Church as it comes to expression 'at Corinth' and as it reproduces itself 'in your house'; or, in modern terms, between the parish Church and the house Church.

[1] The substance of an address given to Wells Theological College, November 17, 1949. Reprinted from *Theology*, August 1950.

The parish Church (and, needless to say, I am using 'Church' here and throughout to describe not a building but a community) is something that is familiar enough. But the idea of the house Church is one that needs clarifying.

There are two mistakes we can make in our thinking at this point, both of which derive from an untheological attitude of mind. The first is to think of the house Church as a purely temporary expedient: a makeshift arrangement characteristic of the earliest Church in Jerusalem or in any other mission area, an organization which serves until the parish Church can be constituted. (This line of thinking very soon betrays the insidious identification of the parish Church with a building of bricks and mortar!) And the second error is to think of the house Church simply as an evangelistic weapon, a technique for getting at those on the frontier not yet ready to accept the full Christianity of the parish Church. It is, as it were, a half-way house for the semi-converted—taking Christianity into the home or factory, through which later to pass men on to the full sacramental life of the Church.

But both these conceptions are inadequate in the light of the New Testament. For it, the Church in the house is not an *ad hoc* expedient: it is a theologically necessary part of the life of the body. When St Paul writes: 'Aquila and Prisca, together with the church in their house, send you hearty greetings in the Lord';[1] or, from the other end: 'Greet Prisca and Aquila . . . and the church in their house';[2] or: 'Give my greetings to the brethren at Laodicea, and to Nympha and the church in her house';[3] he is not implying that these people were working in fringe areas where a 'parish' had as yet not been established (the places mentioned are in fact such well settled centres as Ephesus, Rome and Laodicea); nor that these were semi-Christian outposts of the Faith. The implication is, rather, that these were Churches within the 'parish' Church, in much the same way as today the parish Church is a Church within the diocese. Each colony of Christianity was honeycombed with smaller units.[4]

---

[1] I Cor. 16.19.    [2] Rom. 16.3, 5.    [3] Col. 4.15.

[4] It would be a mistake, of course, to look in the New Testament for any clearly defined hierarchical structure of house, parish and diocese. However,

This conception of the cellular structure of each parish, reflecting the cellular structure of each diocese, is something that has been grievously lost in the modern Church. We should never think of a diocese being an agglomeration of individuals or a federation of local organizations (such as the Mothers' Union or the Church Lads' Brigade), but always as an organic union of *parishes*. But on the smaller scale that is precisely how we *are* content to think. Our parishes are for the most part collections of individuals; or, if these are brought together, it is in organizations. These latter are not units of the whole Church in miniature, but sectional groupings founded on some specifically limited basis of sex, age, or interest. No one could possibly call them *Churches*, though they may sometimes try to act like Churches, and we have the theologically dubious practice of corporate Communions for special organizations and societies—as though anything other than a *Church* could celebrate the Eucharist. By contrast, the house Church is essentially of the same mixture as the lump, except that the area of natural community is smaller (e.g., a street) and may, in these days when communities are often not geographical at all, be outside the parish structure altogether (for instance in an office or factory).

I believe that the theological recovery of this idea of 'the Church in the house' is one of the most important tasks of our generation. Whereas the organization is an optional extra, of the *bene esse* of the parish, I believe that the cellular structure of the Church will be rediscovered as a necessity of its life. It was what John Wesley meant when he insisted that every Methodist—that is to say, every methodical Anglican—must be a member of a class meeting. It is the kind of thing that is being reborn, this time outside the parish Church, in the movement of the Spirit

in Col. 4.15f. Paul distinguishes between 'the Church of the Laodiceans' and 'the Church' within it that met at the house of Nympha. In large centres, like Rome, there must have been a number of house Churches (as Rom. 16.5, 14, 15 suggests), which were destined themselves to become the nuclei of later parishes (cf. C. H. Dodd, *Romans*, p. 237, and the quotations given by Sanday and Headlam, *Romans*, p. 421). The exact ecclesiastical organization of the Apostolic or any other age is unimportant. What is of theological significance is the application of the term *the Church*, with all the high doctrine that goes with it, to the smallest unit of Christian existence within the larger whole.

described in *France Pagan?*. But the danger is that we shall miss the real theological significance of it all. It is easy to regard the house Church simply as a technique for evangelism (which in the first place it normally is, since the Church lives not only for the evangelism but by it), and then to go on to say, after reading such a book as *France Pagan?*: 'Yes, but the situation is very different here, and we do not need to employ such drastic methods.' But, whether we need them as techniques for the unconverted or not, to take this attitude may be to miss precisely what God is trying to say to this generation through them—namely, that here is something of theological necessity for the very *esse* of the Church and for the life of every member within it. We have a defective idea of the house Church if we *define* it as something which is a half-way stage to the parish Church. Rather, it is a vital cell within the Body itself, which should be reflecting in microcosm the *whole* life and activity of the community of Holy Spirit—*all* that St Paul meant by describing it as 'the Church', the great Church, in the house.

And within the body it has a function which is irreplaceable. This can be described best, perhaps, in terms of the Johannine metaphor. The house Church represents, so to speak, the tap-roots of the vine, that of the life of the tree most closely in contact with the clinging soil of everyday existence; it is the tree as it is embedded in the deepest crevices and seams of the secular world. The house Church is what feeds new life into the parish Church, as the innumerable tap-roots nourish the stock of the vine. And then, from the parish, the Church can throw out its leaves and fruit in the great dioceses and provinces which cover the earth, and rear its head in the heavenly places as 'the general assembly and church of the first-born'. But without the house Church it becomes like those trees whose roots are all visible above the ground, which are fast losing living contact with the soil, either to take anything out of it or to put anything back into it.

So far I have simply worked out what I believe to be the theology of the Church in the house. I propose to conclude by illustrating the implications of this in one direction only, which is at once the most obvious and yet to the modern mind the most startling.

The house Church, if it is really the whole Church in micro-cosm, must reproduce in its life all the 'marks' of catholicity—the Apostles' teaching and fellowship, the breaking of bread, and the prayers. The first and the last of these, in the form of groups for Bible study and prayer, are well accepted marks of the Church in the cell. What I want to say will be concerned solely with the second—namely, the breaking of the bread. For the Eucharist is, *par excellence*, the pattern action of the Church, that by which the *Koinonia* is constituted and by which it is to be recognized, whether it be in a cathedral or a prison-camp. One should not be able to come across the Community at any level without finding the Communion.[1]

At once, I suppose, we are faced with the objection: 'But how can a *bit* of the parish celebrate the Holy Communion? How can a few people, a house, take upon themselves the action of the whole Church?' That only goes to show how awry our doctrine of the Church has got. Ask another question: 'How can the

[1] It is impossible from the scanty evidence to be dogmatic about the Eucharist in the house churches of the New Testament. Acts 2.46 ('And day by day, attending the temple together and breaking bread in their homes') may reflect a purely temporary arrangement. But at least it is clear that *kat' oikon* must mean 'at home' or 'in every house' (*i.e.*, each group in its own household) and does not imply that the whole community (of over 3,000 souls) moved round for a corporate Eucharist 'from house to house' (A.V.). There is no direct mention of later house celebrations, but it is most improbable that the house-hold, say, of Philemon did not break bread together eucharistically. Admission to a house as a religious unit would seem to have given the right to meet at its table for the Lord's Supper and to burial in the family vault (*cf.* C. H. Dodd, *Romans*, p. 237). The discussion in 1 Cor. 11 appears to be concerned with what would properly be called the parish Eucharist, though naturally, like every church service till the third or fourth century, it would have occurred in a private house.

The house celebration has always been retained in the Church in some form —e.g. in royal and episcopal chapels. Great houses had their chapels, where celebrations for the household of the Church in that place were allowed, with the proviso that these did not occur on Sundays and festivals and so destroy the parish Eucharist. The mission Church within a parish is, of course, a swollen form of the house Church (as which, indeed, it often started), and some of their deeds of dedication witness to the cellular structure of the parish by stipulating that they shall not be used for celebrations on great festivals.

parish celebrate the Eucharist?' To us that seems obvious. But it was far from obvious to the Church of the second century, which inclined to hold that only the *diocesan* Eucharist, at which the bishop presided, could be valid. But that difficulty was overcome by the recognition that at every Eucharist, at whatever level, the whole Church is celebrating; and hence the stipulation that the president must be a priest, ordained and authorized as he is by the bishop to act in the name of the universal Church of God. It is always *the Church* which celebrates, be it the Church in the diocese, in the parish, or in the house. It is significant that when, on a recent occasion, I spoke of the Christian community celebrating the Eucharist in the house, I was at once suspected of advocating lay celebration. So little do we remember today that the action of the Eucharist is *always* at every level, the Christian community celebrating through the priest, and not the priest celebrating *for* a congregation.

That silent revolution which Dom Gregory Dix has analysed so devastatingly in his essay in the symposium, *The Parish Communion*—namely, the change in the Eucharist from being the action of the whole body of Christ to something done *by* the clergy *for* the laity—is what above all the movement for the parish Communion is concerned to reverse. That is being slowly accomplished at the parish level on Sundays. But for week-day celebrations, the situation remains as it was in the Middle Ages. The low Mass, with the priest celebrating either by himself or for a few individuals, against which the Orthodox Church has always set its face, is universal. The Reformers may have tried to make lay communion compulsory, whereas their predecessors only exhorted it, but, apart from the single act of communion, the service has remained, in Dix's words, 'a purely clerical performance. All that has changed is that instead of offering the sacrifice for the laity the function of the clergy is now to "provide communion" for the laity.'[1]

The only way back is to apply here all the theology of the Sunday parish Communion and to rediscover the week-day Eucharist as the celebration *par excellence* of the Church in the

[1] *The Parish Communion*, p. 138.

house. This would mean that the present individualistic low Mass might gradually come to be superseded by a number of house-celebrations, very probably in the evening, all of which would be gathered up in the parish Communion on Sundays. *Where* these celebrations take place—in the church building or in the home—is largely irrelevant: it is *the community that celebrates them* that is important. But to such an extent have we lost our roots in the soil that the only way to recover the integral connection of the Eucharist with daily work may be to take the whole thing back into the midst of the sweat and muck it is meant to be offering and transforming.

Here are a few lines from a description of a Mass celebrated at the end of a day by a priest-workman in a docker's home in France. 'More beautiful than the flowers (brought by some of the dockers—real flowers from a florist) were the careful but heavy genuflections of this priest who had been working all day at the docks and whose movements evidenced the weights he had been carrying. The mystery of the Redemption is taking place at the very spot where it is needed. Outside, the seven children of the Valès family are playing, and when after our thanksgiving we meet in the court all hung with drying linen and old blankets being aired, life seems new to everyone.'[1]

It is when the Eucharist is taken back into life like that that we shall begin to rediscover many things that we have forgotten. At the parish level, and still more at the cathedral level, it is bound, like every large-scale social action, secular or sacred, to become formal and stylized. That is how it should be. But that is a healthy development only if we are at the same time, at the level of the house Church, knowing something which is not formal but genuinely spontaneous. We should clearly be missing something vital if the only meal we ever knew was a boiled-shirt dinner party or a Lord Mayor's banquet.

What will happen if the Eucharist is really lived back into the everyday soil-stained world only the Holy Spirit can say. I should be surprised, however, if we do not see its reintegration with the *Agape* meal, so that once more the Eucharistic elements

[1] *France Pagan?*, p. 211.

become something taken off the table 'as they were eating'. The special vestments, the special vessels, will either disappear at this level or be radically modified. (Incidentally, if the chalice and paten become the best 'piece' that the household possesses, it may make people realize how unworthy so much modern crockery is of the Lord's table, which is what every Christian table should be —and that goes also for the whole setting and manners of the meal.)

Above all, the liturgy itself, when really taken down, will have to be built up again in a far simpler form to be suitable for the Church in the cell. One could hope perhaps that considerable freedom of experiment might be authorized *at this level*, tied only to the four great 'moments' of the primitive Eucharist, namely, the Offertory, the Thanksgiving, the Fraction, and the Communion. I say *at this level*, for I am convinced that we are not, as a Church, in a position to revise our *parish* liturgy at this moment. That will have to come, if we agree with Dom Gregory Dix that, despite all the efforts of the Reformers to make the Eucharist once more the service of the people, 'Cranmer's Communion Service would seem to be only one instance among many of that "atomized" individualistic piety which was common to the devotion of the Reformation and counter-Reformation alike in the sixteenth century'.[1] That is a hard, and doubtless exaggerated, judgement. It is not my present purpose to argue its justice, but rather to insist that any new Prayer Book revision, whether one thinks it needs to be drastic or not, must come *from below* and not merely from above (as, for instance, it did in 1928). What is going to bring the real changes that are needed is when men see that the liturgy we now have cannot be made adequately to sum up at the parish level on Sunday all that the Eucharist in the cell has come to mean to them on a week-day. There is no need to panic; this will be a process of generations. But it can happen at all only if at the level of the house Church the Holy Spirit is really given free course. Why are we so frightened by this? We believe in sin; have we ceased to believe even more that if the Church is really being the Church it *cannot* go wrong?

[1] *The Parish Communion*, p. 140.

Let me end where I began, by insisting that all this must be seen as a *theological* rediscovery. It is not merely an evangelistic technique, for getting people into the Church, important as it may be even as that. The house Church is *itself* the Church, the Church in the basement, in the smallest possible unit of Christian existence, whether it be among the dockers at Corinth or theological students at Wells. Indeed, a theological college (and particularly perhaps this one with its house structure), so far from being 'above' this sort of thing, would seem to be one of the most obvious places in which to start trying to live out what it means. One has in such an institution a relative independence, and can count, one presumes, on a tolerably high level of theological awareness. And it might be hoped from a centre such as this to contribute by experiment quite a lot to the kind of liturgy appropriate to this basement level of Christian living (though, of course, it would be a very different liturgy from that suitable, say, for a group of dockers).

Finally, a personal experience, for what little it is worth. During the years of its existence a parochial cell of which I was a member did, on one or two occasions, seek to express the pattern of Christian living which we knew together in a cell celebration. It was only a very tentative beginning. It was done in the church building and in what one might call the 'parish' setting, but with an order which, though written for quite another occasion, was composed very largely from the early liturgies to stress the corporate offering. It was essentially an experiment in the Holy Spirit, and went only a very short way. But I think that everyone there those evenings, however they expressed it or could not express it, went away conscious of having been present at something very primitive, almost eschatological, and something which has changed our understanding of the Eucharist ever since. It is perhaps *an* essential element of the Christian Passover that it too should be eaten 'in haste', when there is not the leisure for set ceremonial, but among the tables and chairs of the home, by men who, like the Israelites of old, must go on their way in the morning. Of course there is the place for all the richness and glory of the high Mass, the parish and cathedral Eucharist: indeed, let us make it as rich and colourful as we can. But as we come to it to pray, as we do in this week's collect, for God's 'household the Church' may it vibrate with all those overtones of meaning brought to it by every member of the congregation from the Fellowship as he knows it in the Church of his own house!

This article was destined to touch off vastly more than I ever contemplated. In particular, it coincided with some thinking along much the same lines to which the Reverend Ernest Southcott was being driven by the pressures of his parochial situation in Halton, Leeds. What has happened at Halton since then is now familiar, and has been set out by Ernest Southcott himself in his book, *The Parish Comes Alive* (Mowbrays, 1956). Meanwhile, the need for rediscovering the Church in the house has revealed itself in widely separated parts of the ecumenical movement. The entire number of *Laity* for April 1957, the Bulletin of the Department on the Laity of the World Council of Churches, was devoted to these developments and contains a full bibliography up to that date.

As it sums up things I should still wish to say, I add by way of a postscript my letter to *Theology* in August 1953 which set down my reaction to seeing the house Church in action at Halton for the first time.

In his article in your May issue Mr Southcott referred back to the theological kite that I flew some four years ago and to which you were kind enough to give anchorage in your number of August 1950. Since Mr Southcott's article appeared I have spent a long week-end in his parish at Halton, seeing the visions of which I then dreamed the dreams. As we each started, about the same time, from very different points of view—I from the needs of New Testament theology, he from the pressures of a parish—it might conceivably be of interest to readers of *Theology* to share the second thoughts which the combination has evoked.

I shall not attempt to describe what I saw at Halton, except to say that one found the Church living at a level at which it can seldom have lived since the days of the Acts. The breaking of bread from house to house and the rediscovery of the *ecclesia* of God in all its fullness at basement level—these can be described only by sharing in them and by listening to the unaffected testimony of men and women who owe to them their knowledge of Christ and a churchmanship, vivid and articulate, often concealed from the wise and prudent.

In isolating the fact of the house Church, one must never forget that in Halton this is issuing out of and feeding into the life of a vigorous parish Communion and parish Meeting, itself integrated into the life of the diocese (how often, as here, is the Bishop's name the first thing one reads on the church notice board?). The real significance of this experiment is that it is not a new form of congregationalism, but basic episcopacy. But, confining discussion to the Church in the house, I would pick out three things which look to be emerging of permanent significance for the Church as a whole. None of them is new, but each is coming with the force of an experienced fact, more potent than any amount of theory.

1. The first is a living experience of a *form* of the Church different from that which most people in this country have ever actually known. And it is a form which compels those who find themselves within it to face questions which other levels of Christian living still allow them to evade. When there *is* no church to *go to*, one *can* only *be* the Church. At this level there is a new constraint both towards mission and towards deeper involvement with one's neighbour in Christ. One cannot ignore either the house next door (there is no real 'next door' to the parish church) or the Christian next to one (the parlour is very different from the pew).

In this form of the Church, too, the challenge of disunity comes with fresh force. When most of the *superficial* differences disappear and men of the same household still find themselves divided, the 'why?' and the 'how long?' press with more insistent reality. At the same time there is being built up in the house Church something much less vulnerable to disintegration from *without*. In the event of persecution the Church does not have to go underground: it *is* underground, even if the superstructure has to go.

2. The second thing that is being discovered is the meaning of holiness. By uniting the words 'holy' and 'common', hitherto defined as opposites, Christianity created something entirely new, and by that juxtaposition the religion of the Word made flesh stands or falls. By taking the Holy Communion from the sanctuary to the scullery, the 'offence' of Christian holiness is once more made unequivocal. Is a consecrated building the only 'right' place for the Sacrament? That is instinctively felt by those who still doubt the house celebration. But all who have shared in it are unanimous that in fact nothing of reverence is lost, but rather that henceforth the most common is sensed as holy. 'I now feel my house is really a bit of God's world'; 'I can't just chuck my things around anyhow in this room now'; 'We find we can't quarrel over the table on which the Holy Communion has been celebrated.' The relation of work to worship no longer appears as the integration of two foreign things.

The *forms* of this newly found holiness, the media through which at this level Holy Communion is most naturally expressed, have still largely to be discovered. But if it is to have a chance of spontaneous growth it must be allowed its own liberty. As I see it, it will be a pity if those in authority, from caution or administrative tidiness, apply here the canons of liturgical expression on which they would rightly insist for the parish Eucharist.

3. The third question that is being thrown up is the nature and future of the ministry. On many other grounds—of manpower, economics, and evangelism—the need for a supplemental non-professional ministry is gaining recognition. Indeed, in some form this seems inevitable if the Church of England is not to be in for an indefinite period of retrenchment. The real fear is that nothing will be done till it is economically inescapable. That will only prove the Marxists right and deprive the Church of any spiritual advantage she might reap from it.

The significance of the house Church is that it raises this question precisely in the right form and with immediate urgency. It shows a new type of ministry to be a necessary requirement of the normal (parochial) form of the Church's mission and not merely of evangelistic adventures that might (very wrongly) be dismissed as side-lines or stunts. It shows the real need to be not mere assistants at the parish Church (lay readers, permanent deacons, etc.), but breakers of bread, priests, of indigenous Churches. The urgency can be stated quite simply by saying that from this month Halton will be without a single assistant priest. A movement of the Spirit like this, because it is fully catholic, is bound always to be tied to the ministry; must it be constantly at its mercy?

The compass of a letter prevents one from stating the principles or making the qualifications which are necessary to guard against misunderstanding. The experiment is full of dangers and short-comings, of which those are most conscious who are most deeply quickened. But I should like to put on record for what it is worth —and I measure my words carefully—that I believe this development of the Church in the house to be the single most important new thing that is happening in the Church of England today.

CHAPTER SIX

# Intercommunion and Concelebration[1]

IN THE COURSE OF its valuable report submitted to the Evanston Assembly of the World Council of Churches, *Our Oneness in Christ and our Disunity as Churches*, the section on Faith and Order pleaded for a deeper exploration of 'the implications of the one Baptism for our sharing in the one Eucharist'. It did not itself, however, offer any further suggestions in this direction. This paper is simply an attempt to carry through the theological principles set out in the Report, in the belief that they do in fact afford a real hope of breaking the deadlock that appears to have been reached in this matter of the relation between Baptism and Eucharist, Unity and Intercommunion. What follows was in its original form a memorandum submitted to the Committee appointed by the Church of England to comment on the Faith and Order Report. I should emphasize that the views expressed in it are entirely my own, though the Committee did see fit to include it as an appendix to its own findings.

The present situation could be summarized by saying that there are, on the one hand, those who look to intercommunion as the *expression* of unity achieved, while on the other, there are those who regard it also as a *means* to the achievement of that unity. The presupposition of the first is that intercommunion is impossible until there is a unity, alike of faith and of order, which it can genuinely express. The presupposition of the second is that intercommunion is one of the most powerful means towards such union, and as such must not be denied even now.

The theology of the Report in fact judges both these presuppositions. For what the Eucharist does is not to express the

[1] Reprinted from *The Ecumenical Review*, ix: 3, April 1957.

empirical unity of the Church, whether now or in the future; nor must communion be judged simply by whether or not it does in fact promote this unity. What the Eucharist does is always to bring to us, and bring upon us, the *perfect* unity of *Christ*, both that primal unity which is ours in the finished work of Christ and that eschatological unity of the one new Man made whole in him. Every Eucharist is an *anamnesis* of the one and a forestallment of the other. In each case it makes present and brings to us a unity which empirically *does not exist* except in a gravely distorted reflection. The mistake arises when we allow our attitude to intercommunion to be determined, not by reference to *this* unity, but solely by reference to the greater degree of empirical unity which we see ahead of us: *when* this greater unity does come, or *if* thereby it can come, then intercommunion becomes justified.

But in fact at *every* stage in the Church's earthly pilgrimage the Eucharist will be presenting and anticipating a unity which empirically does not exist. The sole test is not whether or not we are sufficiently united to *express our* unity by 'coming together to one place', but whether we are united enough to *bear Christ's* unity by receiving to ourselves and upon ourselves what we are not—or, rather, what we are and fail to be. For by eating and drinking we deliberately take to ourselves the one Body which we find we cannot be.

This awareness of the fact of judgement is the truth behind the position (falsely formulated) that we cannot communicate together until there is a unity to express. The other position (though formulated again in terms simply of a future empirical unity) preserves the equally important Pauline thesis that the Eucharist *creates* us as the one Body we find we cannot be. Neither of these principles must be emphasized to the exclusion of the other. On the one hand, casual communion, whether of a Church or individual, is sinful and terrible in its consequences, as Paul warned the Corinthians. And yet the Church cannot any more than the individual, let the fact of judgement—that it is not yet 'good' or united enough—prevent it from receiving the sole thing which can make it what it is not. The test is not: 'Have we sufficient unity yet to *express*?' but, 'As the broken Body, which within

D

this age we must ever in some degree remain, dare we receive the whole Body?' Dare we say *together*, 'Come, Lord Jesus!' Or dare we go on saying it *apart*? In which lies the greater sin? We must always be prepared to ask both questions with equal seriousness—and not simply the first.

One practical point here requires to be put in perspective. It is often argued, particularly in the Church of England, that we *cannot* in any case break the bread together until we have a single, or mutually recognized, ministry, and that we are compelled therefore to wait for the greater degree of empirical unity which is marked by this stage. This allows one element in our manifold dividedness to have an absolute or overriding effect. The principle of judgement *is* permitted at this point to operate to the exclusion of the other principle. This is to give the ordained ministry of the Church an absolute significance or veto over the rest of the life of the Church that theologically it cannot possess: it is to subordinate the Church to the ministry, and not the ministry to the Church, which is the only true order. The decision on intercommunion must not be allowed to be determined by one element in our division alone—though the dividedness of the ministry is, of course, one of the major points of judgement under which we stand and which must be taken into account when we examine and judge ourselves, that we be not condemned.

But, *if* we decide that to break the bread together is in a given situation less sinful than to break the bread separately, and if we cannot do that through a single ministry, then the question arises whether we should not, and indeed must not, do it jointly through our existing ministries *together*—in other words, by concelebration. This seems to me a very important proposal, both theologically and practically, which, as far as I know, has scarcely been considered by Faith and Order (it received no mention in the Lund volume on *Intercommunion*). This is not the place in which to go into the history and theology of the idea of concelebration, which, from practical experience, I believe to merit much more examination in this context than it has received. I call attention to it here simply because the failure to see any way round the impasse of our divided ministries has in practice contributed to giving this fact a *theological* priority and empirical veto that I believe it has no right to possess. And it has played into the hands of the false premise that when, but only when, we have solved this issue (or, indeed, any other given issue of faith or order) there will then be a sufficient unity to find *expression* in intercommunion.

All this raises the question whether we should not re-examine our attitude to intercommunion and unity, and ask ourselves if it has not been formulated too much in legal rather than theological categories, with the natural desire for administrative tidiness playing its usual part. The clear-cut division between episcopal and non-episcopal ministries, though itself a schism of major *theological* significance, has, I believe, been allowed, at any rate for many Anglicans, to become a legal obstacle behind which it has been possible to shelter from any other theological thinking in regard to this issue. If we cannot in any case have intercommunion until the question of orders is settled, we can meanwhile absolve ourselves from thinking out the theological conditions in which this becomes less sinful than separate communions.

Since, moreover, the issue of Orders is one that can be settled only at the level of the Churches as a whole, it means that there cannot be intercommunion between any groups or congregations until there is intercommunion between their respective denominations. The degree of unity and the pressure for unity in the *local* situation—which are the spiritual realities that must finally decide whether the common Table or the separated Table is the greater hypocrisy—cannot be allowed to make any difference at all. In a great number, alas the majority, of parishes the local churches and chapels are indeed still so divided that to invoke, through intercommunion, the one Body that their lives deny could only deepen our guilt. Let us admit that—with shame. But it is the rigidity of the present position which is leading to frustration or indiscipline, where local Churches in many matters deeply at one become convinced that it is already more sinful *for them* always to celebrate apart than ever to celebrate together. Is there no solution for them except disloyalty to their Church as a whole?

I happen to be in a situation, in a college chapel, where the pressure, which would otherwise be intolerable, can in fact legally find outlet in intercommunion. What I would plead for, on the theological grounds so admirably stated in the Evanston Report, is a greater flexibility, which would allow different points of the front to go forward at their own (or, may we say, at God's?) pace, without everything being held up until integration of the ministry is finally achieved. And the way in which I would visualize this happening, at any rate in England, is not by further extension of the Convocation Resolutions of January 1933 (that is, by more 'open' Anglican celebrations, which are theologically and pastorally unsatisfactory, because not reciprocal) but by concelebration. This recognizes quite openly that until integration we still require a plurality of ministries to break together the one loaf which, for all our disunity, has yet the power to make us one Body.

Once released from the stranglehold which the division of the ministry has been allowed to impose, we should be free to face as a whole the spiritual and theological conditions which make united communion both possible and, may be, imperative. The last thing I should wish to suggest is that the schism between our ministries is not a major, perhaps the major, rift in the Body which causes us to eat judgement when we feed upon the un-divided Body. Indeed, the very necessity for the presence of at least two ministers in order that the Body of Christ in any given place may receive the sacrament of unity is a reminder, not a cloaking, of the judgement involved. But at least it does open the way for mercy to rejoice over judgement. And that mercy is the supreme divine reality to which our oneness in Christ, despite our disunity as Churches, is the constant and marvellous testimony.

# CHAPTER SEVEN

# Episcopacy and Intercommunion[1]

THE SLAP IN THE face of the Church of England recently administered by the Kirk[2] has its sad as well as its salutary aspect. It is a grim prospect for those who care deeply about the ecumenical movement that any effective steps towards closer union have probably been put off for a generation. It is sad, if only because the passions aroused by the so-called 'Bishops' Report'—itself a real achievement in ecumenical theology—have had so little to do with theology. But I believe it will also turn out to be salutary. So rude a jolt may well have been necessary in order to make us think again. And this may soon become imperative. For in the Church of England we have full-scale negotiations with the Methodists on our hands, and it would be tragic if they went the same way. And there is a real possibility that they might, since we are here negotiating in much the same spirit, and could easily run into the same difficulties.

A reappraisal may indeed be being forced upon us of the whole present round of reunion discussions. This goes back now some thirteen years, to the Cambridge University sermon preached by the Archbishop of Canterbury on November 3, 1946, which he entitled 'A Step Forward in Church Relations'. No sermon delivered since the War has probably had such far-reaching consequences, and few can doubt that it has marked 'a step forward'. It has released a new impetus and provided a limited objective which has made constructive discussion possible. Its

[1] Reprinted from *Theology*, October 1959.

[2] *Relations between Anglican and Presbyterian Churches*. The uncompromising rejection of the General Assembly of the Church of Scotland in May 1959 of the Report.

essential proposal was that we should take two bites at the cherry
of reunion, aiming first not at complete constitutional union but
at full intercommunion, this latter to be achieved by the non-
episcopal Churches 'taking episcopacy into their systems'.

I believe it has done nothing but good to give this imaginative
proposal the testing it deserved. For it is only by taking it as far
as it can go that the dangers in it have begun to be apparent. But
having now sighted them, I believe that we should be prepared to
draw up sharply, before we become involved in another crash
which, because it is nearer home, could set things back even more
disastrously.

Since the immediate danger is focused in the conversations
between the Church of England and the Methodists, it will be
best to concentrate on these rather than rake over the Presbyterian
wreck. The immediate aim of these conversations, as the Interim
Report[1] makes clear, is not the union of our two Churches but
the achievement of intercommunion between them. To this end
—which it is stressed is only a half-way house—the Report
explores the ways in which the Methodists might become an
episcopal Church. While everyone agrees that 'nothing short of
organic unity . . . should be the final goal', it is open to serious
question whether this is in fact the best first step towards it.

To explore means of unifying episcopal and non-episcopal
ministries so that we may become one Church is something to
which we should be prepared to give, and to sacrifice, a very
great deal. To go through this exercise in order that we may
for the foreseeable future have parallel and competing episcopal
denominations would appear to get us very little further. It means,
it is true, that we should be able to communicate and to celebrate
at each other's tables. But this, if we still have no real desire for
*union*, may be just as sinful as to refrain from so doing. 'If there is
a real passion for unity', Bishop Lesslie Newbigin has written,[2]
'and a willingness to pay the cost of it, intercommunion is the
proper relationship of the Churches as they move forward to the

---

[1] *Conversations between the Church of England and the Methodist Church: An
Interim Statement*, 1958 (reviewed, editorially, in *Theology*, September 1958).

[2] 'Anglicans and Christian Reunion', *Theology*, June 1958, p. 225.

fulfilment of their unity. But experience surely shows that inter-communion apart from any such passion merely slackens the tension of desire, and weakens the sense of seriousness of what is involved in sharing together in the Lord's Supper. If, in one street, we have episcopal church No. 1 (Anglican), episcopal church No. 2 (Presbyterian), and episcopal church No. 3 (Method-ist), each under a different bishop, related to a quite separate church organization, it is hard to see that the scandal of division has in any way been lessened in that street, even though the members are free to drop in at each other's communions'. Full communion without union with a distant Church, as in South India, or even in Scotland, may be a highly desirable step—so that when a member or a minister moves from one to the other there is no break. But for disunited and competing Churches *in the same parish* to claim to be in full communion with each other is to invite the world, not to believe in our unity, but to question our integrity.[1]

Moreover, to use the historic episcopate to compass this end is in danger of evacuating it of the very meaning for which I as an Anglican cherish it and would yearn for Methodists to share it. Either the local bishop is, as Ignatius insisted, the centre and focus in any given place of the one catholic Church, or he is nothing worth contending for. That in one town there should be two—or three or four—local bishops each claiming, and acknowledged by the others, to represent *the* historic episcopate seems if any-thing worse than having one whom half the Christians in the place do not recognize. Let us go all out to achieve a single ministry which is truly catholic and which all acknowledge. Let us beware, as a supposed half-way house to that, of multiplying episcopates. If the bishop is the focus of the catholic Church in any one place, then there cannot be two bishops any more than two catholic Churches. The proposal we are asked to consider is in danger of countenancing precisely the situation which everyone deplores in

[1] A comparable situation has arisen with the Old Catholics in Holland, where in some places the Church of England is ministering not only to its own ex-patriates but to natives of the country. The Old Catholics have rightly ques-tioned what the agreement on full communion in these circumstances really means.

the Nandyal area of South India, where because of failure to unite there have had temporarily to be parallel episcopates, of the Church of South India and of the Church of India, Pakistan, Burma and Ceylon, Churches which are themselves in communion with each other. Of course, the motives in the two cases are very different: in England such parallel episcopates would be the result of co-operation rather than of schism. Moreover, the Report envisages that this parallelism would exist within a real measure of unity. But when we ask what this unity means, the gathering in general and local assembly of which it speaks amounts to no more than a closely-knit council of Churches. There certainly would not be one bishop in one place.

I am not convinced, as I said, that this is a very profitable pursuit upon which to bend our energies. The Free Churches themselves have long enjoyed such a degree of intimacy without being driven any nearer to organic union. But this does not in itself make it a dangerous pursuit. What makes it dangerous, as the crash in Scotland has shown, is that this very order of procedure forces us into the position of commending episcopacy on the wrong grounds. We find ourselves having to argue it, not as the basis of unity, but as the condition of intercommunion.

Few responsible Christian leaders today would dispute that in some form the historic episcopate is the only practicable basis —to put it no higher—for the reunion of Christendom. That the possession or acquisition of episcopacy is the condition of intercommunion is, I believe, much more questionable Anglican teaching, both historically and theologically. The Lambeth Quadrilateral (of Bible, Creeds, Sacraments and Bishops) was formulated as a basis of unity, an attempted expression of the fulness of the Church: it has come in these latter years to be used as a pre-condition of intercommunion, a minimum qualification of catholicity.[1]

Along this line one soon gets to the position, not that if the

[1] In a comparable way, the rubric requiring Confirmation as the normal prerequisite of Communion has been turned from being a domestic discipline of the Church of England into a fence against Non-conformists. It is reassuring at any rate that the Report refuses to envisage episcopal Confirmation as a necessary condition of intercommunion.

Church is to be one it must be episcopal, but that if a Church is to be a Church at all it must have bishops. Episcopacy comes to be commended not as the source and symbol of unity but as a gimmick for validating sacraments—and this is what neither Presbyterians nor Methodists nor any other non-episcopal Church will stand *or ought to stand.* As long as we make jumping the episcopal hurdle the condition of intercommunion rather than the basis of union we are inevitably committed to commending it on false grounds. And it is not surprising that the hurdle is kicked over.

Moreover, as long as the Church of England shelters behind this hurdle, we shall never be forced to ask ourselves what is the *true* condition of intercommunion. It is worth trying to define what this is, since we have relieved ourselves of the necessity of doing so by taking cover behind the legal obstacle of episcopal orders. Indeed, one of the disconcerting features of the Report is that it concentrates entirely on removing this obstacle, on the assumption apparently that when intercommunion is lawful it is automatically expedient.

The condition of intercommunion, most simply stated, is that a situation is reached in which it becomes more sinful *not* to break a common loaf than to do so. To do so when the one loaf corresponds with no spiritual reality is indeed to invoke judgement upon ourselves, by receiving the very thing our lives deny, the Body of Christ, the one new man in Christ Jesus. And, let us be frank, this is still the situation in the majority of parishes in England today, where the congregations of the different denominations are perfectly content to go on in their separated ways. Indiscriminate intercommunion in these circumstances would be sin, *and would continue to be so even if the other denomination were episcopal.* But where the spiritual reality does exist, then to refuse a common loaf is to be guilty of acting an equal lie. This the Church of England has long recognized in its permission for opening Communion to non-Anglicans in a college chapel,[1]

[1] This freedom was regularized by the Upper Houses of the Convocations of Canterbury and York in January 1933, but it was not created then. In composite resolutions of both Convocations, defining the conditions and occasions of limited intercommunion at Anglican altars, the clauses relating to

where its members meet at one table for everything else and are to all intents and purposes a single spiritual community.

Such is the condition of intercommunion. It may be negated by a number of things, including a deep division on church order. But it is essentially a spiritual condition, and it will vary widely in local situations. To require an episcopally ordained ministry as the *sine qua non* of any intercommunion is not only to allow the ministry an absolute veto over all the rest of the Church's life to which it has no theological right; it is to impose a strait jacket which prevents advance at any point on the front till all have achieved it. Since ministries can be unified only at the level of denominations as a whole, nothing can be done from the bottom till something is done at the top. Already there are situations in which this is producing fearful frustration. Indeed, I could not have answered for the spiritual state of the college chapel of which till recently I have been Dean, had we not had the privilege of which I have spoken.

But even this privilege extends only to the sharing by members of other Churches in an Anglican celebration. In an Anglican foundation, such as an Oxford or Cambridge college, where there is no other celebration, this provision is adequate. But in a parish it is far from satisfactory, because there can be no reciprocity. And the refusal to permit Anglicans to participate in the celebrations of non-episcopal Churches will always carry with it the imputation that we are denying their orders and sacraments, however much we go on asserting that they are equally 'within the Body'. And it is this double talk, as Bishop Newbigin said in the same article, and as the Scots have said less politely since, which is fast earning us the reputation of perfidious Anglicans.

But there is no need for any lack of candour. Is it not possible to accept without pretence the situation as it actually is? The position in many places is that we can, and indeed must, spiritually speaking, break one loaf, but that we cannot at present do it

---

school and college chapels provoked no controversy. In fact, the sole reference to it in the speeches was in Archbishop Lang's summing up in the Convocation of Canterbury, when he made it clear that this clause was simply giving official recognition to long-established practice.

through a single mutually acknowledged ministry. Then should we not do it through our divided ministries together? Con-celebration, with two (or more) ministers presiding at the table on behalf of the congregations they represent, meets those Anglicans who conscientiously believe that it is not a valid Eucharist unless celebrated by a priest; and at the same time it accepts as joint celebrant one who is in no way asked to deny the fulness of the ministry he has received.[1]

This is an interim arrangement, which indeed *solves* nothing; but equally it hides nothing. Indeed, to quote some words of an earlier article in which I argued the case more fully,[2] 'the very necessity for the presence of at least two ministers in order that the Body of Christ in any given place may receive the sacrament of unity is a reminder, not a cloaking, of the judgement involved. But at least it does open the way for mercy to rejoice over judgement'. And that, where the situation is ripe, is a saving necessity.

For it is by partaking of the one loaf that we, who are many, are made one Body. That is the essential truth enshrined in the Archbishop's proposal that intercommunion should be seen as the means to union and not merely as the fruit of it. And the validity of that truth has been reinforced for me beyond any contradiction by the experience over the past eight years of being able to break one bread in a college chapel: this joint participation made us one as nothing else could. What is not nearly so clear is that we should attempt to use what is properly the basis of union as a means of making such intercommunion possible. If we are not yet ready to unite our Churches, then to unite our ministries so that meanwhile we can enjoy intercommunion involves, as Bishop Newbigin remarked, 'an abandonment of the great truth in this realm to which Anglicanism has borne witness, namely, the indissoluble relation between sacramental fellowship and the total

---

[1] Even in a college chapel there would be much to be said for acknowledging that this is now a genuinely ecumenical community by the appointment of a Free Church Chaplain to work, and concelebrate, with the Anglican Dean required by statute.

[2] 'Intercommunion and Concelebration', *The Ecumenical Review*, April 1957, pp. 263-6. See above, pp. 96-100.

life of the Church'.[1] And to demand episcopacy as the deposit on the ecclesiastical 'never never' is to devalue episcopacy (even if the deposit were to be paid, which it won't be) with no guarantee of ultimate union.

Nothing lasting will be achieved till we cease to be separated Churches, with an integrated ministry and a new freedom in unity such as South India has discovered. Let us back with our prayers, and with our pressure, those who are conversing on our behalf if they really go for the big thing. But if we *are* to have an interim stage, then let it be one that really challenges the local congregation to unity. If there were two congregations, however episcopal, meeting at separate tables within a single college it would be intolerable—and the non-Christians would never believe we were one. Ultimately, as Bishop Newbigin insisted again, the only convincing test of unity is that the Christian family in any one place should visibly be seen to *be* one family, breaking one loaf. And it is here too that the real cost comes. But this is not the cost that the present proposals for intercommunion force us to face. They ask us (or, let us be honest, they ask the Methodists) whether we are prepared for certain changes in church order, in order that we can go on living separately, in however close relations.

Let us negotiate for unity, not for intercommunion, at the top. But meanwhile let us press forward *through intercommunion* from below. Let the one loaf in the one place, the one common Christian life, *despite* our divisions on order, be the spiritual reality that compels us to a common structure and a common episcopacy. If we begin by duplicating bishops, then I have a fear that nothing very urgent will drive us to union. But once a sufficient number of congregations know themselves so close in Christ and his work that they *cannot but* break one loaf, even through our divided ministries, then the demand for a single ministry and a single Church cannot be far behind.

A more promising way forward than that outlined in the Report has since been provided by the proposed establishment,

[1] *Op. cit.*, p. 225. Cf. T. F. Torrance in *Essays in Anglican Self-criticism* (ed. D. M. Paton), pp. 202–5.

at the suggestion of the Archbishop of Canterbury and the leaders of the Methodist Church, of a shared church in the new housing area of Greenhill, Kent. In a letter to *The Times*[1] the Vicar and the Superintendent Methodist minister said: 'We have agreed to alternate Mattins and Methodist morning service, Evensong and Methodist evening service on alternate Sundays, with the Anglican Holy Communion service on Sunday morning at or before 9 a.m. Both denominations will use the Methodist Hymn Book, and Anglicans and Methodists will be welcomed at the services of the other.' Intercommunion is not at the moment in question. But can anyone doubt that the demand for it will become insistent, if the two congregations really grow together in the Spirit? In such a situation concelebration would seem the obvious answer to an otherwise intolerable frustration. And, as another joint letter to *The Times* said,[2] if this is the way forward in an expanding area, why not in 'the immediate and infinitely larger problem of inter-church relationships presented by the "established" area?'.

It is a sign of real hope that the heart of the problem of inter-communion should have shifted from the admission of *individuals* to the sacrament in isolated or occasional situations (though this, of course, remains a genuine problem) to the coming together of Christian *congregations* to know themselves as the Body of Christ in any given place. This restates the issue in its normative and properly corporate terms, opens the way to fresh understanding of the one loaf, and points us, I believe, a new path to unity.

[1] June 29, 1959.    [2] July 6, 1959.

# CHAPTER EIGHT

# The Gospel and Politics[1]

THE DISADVANTAGE OF coming last in a course is that everybody by now, including the preacher, has begun to wonder whether there is anything left to be said. And in a sense the answer to the question 'No religion in politics?' is so obvious that one might wonder whether there was anything to be said anyhow. 'No *religion* in politics?' The alternative is to turn over politics entirely to non-Christians. 'No religion in *politics*?'—but if religion does not come into the ordering of human society then where does it come in? The question is one that answers itself, a rhetorical flourish for church notice-boards. And yet you have only to announce a course of sermons with such a title for there to be a great wagging of heads and flutter of reporters. The subject is hot, and anyone who touches it is conscious of handling something very prickly.

Why is this? Partly, of course, because the word of religion in politics is bound to be a prophetic word, and prophets make us all feel uncomfortable. As was said in a sermon earlier in this course, 'When a man argues that the Church mustn't interfere in politics, it is a safe guess that he belongs to a lucky minority and is not quite sure that the luck will hold'. And vested interest linked to anxiety is one of the most prickly things there is.

But there are other reasons too. We in this country are properly very sensitive about the relation of the Church to party politics. We have seen what has happened to politics on the Continent and what has happened in our own past when the Church gets identified too closely with a party line. And we are rightly

[1] The substance of a sermon preached in St Paul's Cathedral, London, September 30, 1956.

careful about saying things in the name of the Church where Christians are sincerely divided. What I say as a priest from the pulpit must not be simply what I would say as an individual Christian. Few things cut deeper into an Englishman's conscience than ecclesiastics telling him how to vote (though it is apparently quite proper if an archbishop tells the Leader of the Opposition that he should not have divided the House at all. That is statesmanship, not politics; and bipartisanship always looks somehow more Christian).

But there is a still deeper reason why what appears so self-evident, taking religion into politics, is so controversial. That is because most of us are only half-converted to the justification for it, and we take out our uneasiness on other people. Jesus and Paul, we remember, refused to become involved in politics; and if we were really Christians should we not be concentrating on something else? Is the Christian centre of gravity in this world at all? And is what you can achieve by act of Parliament really *our* business? Wasn't Christ concerned with changing individuals not institutions? There are a number of supplementaries, too, about methods, about politics being a dirty business, and the use of force, which occur to us quickly enough; but let us concentrate on the main issue. What is the biblical basis for involvement in politics at all? This is the aspect on which I have been asked to concentrate.

But notice that I said the biblical basis, and not merely the New Testament basis. For precisely the trouble so often is that we isolate the teaching and example of Jesus. We lift him out of the stream of history, and then conclude that he was not involved in it—and that we need not be either.

But Jesus came, as he himself makes abundantly clear, as the last word of a response to God in history, which he was there not to negate but to fulfil. What that response was had been hammered out in the blood and sweat of the Old Testament story. We can sum it up as the meeting of two requirements.

The first is what William Temple described[1] as a 'decision for the God who acts'. The mark which distinguished Israel from all the other nations was the understanding of God, not merely as

[1] In *What Christians stand for in the Secular World.*

the Lord of nature, like the Baalim of the surrounding tribes, but as the Lord of history—a God who does things not in cycles but on a single purposive line. And responsibility to the God of history meant, as those who served him discovered, taking responsibility *for* history. They could no longer be indifferent to where it was going or leave it to others as something alien. They were compelled to enter the power struggle because it was there that the battle for God's control of the world was fought out. Historical absenteeism was simply atheism.

This obedience to God as the God of history can be seen focused in the figure of Moses. Moses could have lived a quiet life with nature looking after the flocks of his father-in-law; but he risked his career and his skin in organizing a brick-layers' strike; and he went on to see through one of the most prolonged and bitter movements for national liberation. Makarios had nothing on him when it came to power politics and Nasser would have found his match in negotiation. Yet here was the man of whom it was said that he 'knew God face to face' and was 'very meek, more than all men who are on the face of the earth'. Religion and politics did not pull in two directions; they were one response. And we see the same combination in Nehemiah, with his trowel in one hand and his sword in the other, building the wall, the highly political wall, round the new state of Israel. These were men who did not go into politics for what they could get out of it: they went in because they knew that to be out of it was to be out of, and disobedient to, what God was doing.

That was the first response required of Israel—'decision for the God who acts'. The second was what Temple called 'decision for neighbour'—for the poor and the stranger, the fatherless and widow. And this was both the complement of the first and its corrective. The complement, since responsibility for history, if it is not just a cliché, means commitment to persons, and the over-riding conviction that 'people matter'. And it was the corrective or check upon it, because politics becomes 'power politics' precisely at the point where persons cease to matter. That is what Nathan had to say to David about Uriah the Hittite, when he hoped to get him forgotten in the army; that is what Elijah had to say to Ahab, when Naboth resisted a compulsory purchase order and was swept aside. That is what Amos and Hosea, Micah and Jeremiah had to go on saying, in season and out of season, to those who held political and economic power. But never did they imply that to hold power was in itself wrong. On the contrary, to suppose that without it you could judge the cause of the fatherless or widow or see that the poor man had his right was manifest hypocrisy. Again, for the Prophets, no more than for Moses, was politics an affair simply of this world, a distraction from religion. Rather, the decision for neighbour went to the very heart of a man's response to God. Listen to Jeremiah addressing the ne'er-do-well son of Josiah, who has succeeded him as King of Judah: 'Woe to him who builds his house by unrighteousness, and his upper rooms by injustice; who makes his neighbour serve him for nothing, and does not give him his wages; who says, "I will build myself a great house with spacious upper rooms", and cuts out windows for it, panelling it with cedar, and painting it with vermilion. Do you think you are a king because you compete in cedar? Did not your father . . . do justice and righteousness? Then it was well with him. He judged the cause of the poor  and needy. . . . *Is not this to know me? says the Lord*' (Jer. 22.13-16). Here right politics *is* religion: it *is* what to *know* the God of history means.

But what happens when we come to the New Testament? Don't we leave this world completely behind? True, the circumstances have changed. Israel is no longer a self-governing state. Jesus, like John the Baptist before him and St Paul after him, has no voice in the political or economic order. And, like the Prophets, they repudiate any attempt to obtain one by force. But it is not only the circumstances that we feel have changed. And we are right. Jesus is the new Moses not the old one (a fact that Archbishop Makarios' actions do not always make clear). For Jesus, the road to freedom follows more closely the other Old Testament pattern of liberation—that of the second Isaiah, the way of the Servant, of power crucified and transfigured. Again, Jesus is the new Moses in his concern for neighbour. The question 'Who is my neighbour?' is radically revalued. The old Moses trusted to legislation to define and implement a man's respon-sibility—and never was there a code more gracious or more exacting than that of Deuteronomy. But Jesus' requirements go beyond any legislation. As Paul saw, for or against such things there is no law.

The circumstances have changed and the level has been in-comparably deepened; but the two basic decisions, for the God who acts and for neighbour, have not been rescinded. The whole burden of Jesus' message, which he can support to its end only by his death, is precisely of the coming of the kingdom of God into history. And that throws him willynilly, as the bearer of the Kingdom, into the very midst of the political struggle, to the extent of being hanged between two insurrectionaries—to all the world as one more of them. 'The Word was made flesh and dwelt among us': the process of identification with history can go no further. And equally the identification with neighbour can get no nearer: for 'whatever you have done to the least of these you have done to *me*'.

But all this, it may seem, is still a far cry from politics, or getting religion mixed up with rates and rent-control. But is it? 'Is not this to know me, saith the Lord?', said the Prophet. And when Jesus said the same even more personally in the great parable of the final judgement, what was 'this'? What was it the doing or leaving undone of which involved knowing or failing to know the Son of man? It was quite simply being concerned for food, for water supplies, for housing and hospitals and prisons. And if in our day you really think you can be concerned for these things, or rather for your neighbour in them, merely at the level of personal kindness and without being drawn into politics, then you are simply being escapist. Certainly your neighbour is not likely to think so. Of course we cannot. And the sooner as Christians we abandon the lingering idea that we can, the sooner we shall get down to facing the real question, and perhaps the only question we shall be asked at the Last Judgement, which is, · quite simply: 'How much have you loved?' No one can say that that is not a question of Jesus; and no one can say that it is not a question of politics. It is the first question we should accustom ourselves to putting to everything we read in the paper or hear on the news. 'Two more Greek terrorists in Cyprus were executed at dawn this morning'. How much have you loved? The question in itself makes no political judgement: the world being what it is, we being what we are, it may, God forgive us, have been unavoidable. It leads to no slick answer which implies that anyone who comes down on the other side cannot be a Christian. The words of Jesus, 'Man, who set me over you to judge and to arbitrate?', must always be remembered: he is not there to give a quick answer to our questions. We are there to give a slow—indeed a life-long—answer to his question: 'How much have you loved?' And for the New Testament, as for the Old, that terrible, searching, political, question is but a hair's breadth from the other and most personal of all questions, 'Peter, John, Mary, . . . lovest thou *me*?'

# CHAPTER NINE

# The Gospel and Race[1]

IN THE COURSE OF that remarkable novel of South African life, *Blanket Boy's Moon*, the very fallible hero, a Basuto African, saves the life of a Mohammedan in the Durban riots and comes under the influence of his religion. Later he speaks to his son of the thing he had discovered in Islam—a real and true equality.

> Libe said eagerly: 'Not like the Christians, O my father, where the white men stay in one church, and make coloured Christians worship in another!'
> 'Not like the Christians, my son! Amongst the Muslims there is nothing of that sort. In the mosque, if the rich man comes in late, there is no place reserved for him—should the one to arrive before him be a beggar, then must he stand on the beggar's left!'
> Alfred said: 'Ee! Monare—that is the religion for us Africans!'

I am not concerned with whether that is a fair picture either of Christianity or of Mohammedanism. I use it simply to introduce the explosive issue of racial equality, and to provoke some serious thought on its precise relation to the Christian gospel. On what grounds as Christians do we take a stand, and what should that stand be?

Many will dismiss these as questions they feel they have already answered. Racial discrimination is obviously a 'bad thing', and they are disposed to leave it at that. In practice, this means that they adopt a general humanitarian attitude of being 'agin' the colour bar, *apartheid*, and the rest, but that their actual judgements

[1] Reprinted from *The Church of England Newspaper*, July 24, 1953.

are determined by their temperament or their political bias.

In the case of non-Christians this is what one might expect. But it becomes more serious when Christians make their judgements on similar grounds, with resulting confusion and even mutual recrimination within the Church. The stand taken by *Christian Action* on South Africa provides an obvious example of how divisive this issue can be even among Churchmen.

I would suggest the main reason for this is that we have not stopped to think at all deeply what really is the Christian foundation for our attitude towards race. Above all, I am convinced that if we were really biblical a situation could not arise where dignitaries of the Church either disavow each other in public or maintain solidarity by elected silence.

First, then, and it is not as obvious a question as it sounds, on what grounds does a Christian take his stand on racial discrimination? Many would answer on the ground of our common humanity—because, in biblical terms, we are all one in Adam. Now it may often be necessary to put it that way in co-operating with non-Christians, but this is not what the New Testament says. In Adam, it asserts, we experience not unity, but enmity, alienation and death. Adam, humanity, was indeed created one in God's image, and we know in our hearts that is what we are made to be; but, as we find it, mankind is rent with division and discord. Out of Adam came Cain and Abel and the tower of Babel. It is precisely from this source that Dr Malan derived his *Herrenvolk* theology which destines the descendants of Ham, supposedly the Negroid races, to perpetual bondage as hewers of wood and drawers of water. That indeed is a tragic isolation and fundamentalist distortion of one element in the Old Testament picture of natural man; but *we have no answer to it* simply by setting against it the other, more liberal one. For they are both equally true, and one cannot prevail over the other. In Adam, apart from Christ, the ideal and the brutal are always at variance, and there is no ground for the reconciliation of the nations.

The basis rather of the Christian position is the fact of the *new* man created in Christ. For to him, in him, they are now already one, and to us they cannot be any different. The New Testament concept of the new humanity is a very profound one. It does not mean simply that all those in the Church are now one in Christ and must live as such. The new man is the whole human race as Christ has claimed it for himself and has given to every member of it a new and equal worth by dying for all without discrimination. The new man, says St Paul whenever he refers to it, *has been created*—it is as objective as the old creation; it is the great new fact of the Christian era. Yet, as is obvious from any glance at the headlines, it is not a finished fact: it is always also in the process of becoming what it is, of acknowledging and accepting its new constitution in Christ. The Church is humanity as it has so far made that acknowledgment, where what Christ has done for the world is accepted in faith and conduct. 'You have put on the new humanity', says St Paul (to give a free translation of Col. 3.10), 'which is yet ever being made new in the acknowledgment of him in whose image it has been created'. The Apostle makes his appeal to the fact of what is objectively true of all men in Christ, and to the fact that the Colossians have accepted for themselves that it *is* true.

If that is the ground on which the Christian takes his stand, what is this stand? Here again I believe we encounter a way of thinking which, because it is unbiblical, does immense damage to the Christian witness. Many talk as if Christians can take different attitudes to racial discrimination, in the same way as they take different attitudes to gambling or politics or the use of force, and that it is thus perfectly possible for them to hold widely diverse and even opposed positions. According to this view, our attitude to race is simply one of many implications of the Gospel, in which some Christians may be more radical than others.

I believe this to be a dangerously false way of looking at it. I am convinced that the whole Christian Gospel stands or falls by our response at this point. For the fact of the new man *is* the very gospel itself. In the Epistle to the Ephesians St Paul describes the single new humanity in which all divisions fall to the ground as itself the very 'mystery of Christ' (3.4-6), the open secret of God in which the Incarnation consists. Christ came precisely that he 'might create in himself the one new man . . . so making peace'

(2.15). Consequently, in the passage from Colossians I quoted earlier as a summary of the Christian position, he at once goes on: 'In this new man it is *impossible* for there to be Greek and Jew, circumcision and uncircumcision, barbarian, Scythian, slave and free man: all is simply—Christ' (3.11).

That does not, of course, mean that in Christ human beings are no longer black and white, male and female, or that they are now equal in endowment or ability. But it does mean that any division or discrimination simply on grounds of race, sex or class is not merely a *bad* thing (a matter of Christian ethics) but impossible for a Christian without denying the very gospel itself.

I suppose most church people in Britain could be brought to acknowledge this in regard to the Communion fellowship—that any such discrimination or exclusion here would be strictly intolerable, in the sense that it would literally make Holy Communion impossible. For this is only what St Paul told the Corinthians, whose sin was simply individualism—eating the food they had brought without waiting to share it with others. For if, he said, you thus show that you have no sense of the Body, it is impossible to eat the Lord's supper: you can receive Communion only to your own damnation. For in Communion you are taking to yourself, inviting upon yourself in judgement, the very thing your conduct denies—the body of Christ, the one new man, the holy community. And there is no Christian gospel left, no Christian community or Communion, where that is denied.

I have taken this instance of the Holy Communion because, as it seems to me, the issue here is absolutely clear and no compromise can be possible. But it is equally impossible without contraction and hypocrisy to limit this to the Communion table. For what we do at Communion is but the pattern for every relationship of our common life—social, economic, political. The utterly revolutionary attitude to slavery, for example, in the Epistle to Philemon, by which the whole institution is undermined from within, cannot remain something which is true only at Communion or even in the small circle of a Christian's personal dealings, though that is where it begins. It must in the end break the institution of slavery as an economic system and find its expression in political legislation. And the same holds of race relations.

Let us be clear. The political issues are incredibly complex, and let no one propose, still less presume to dictate from six thousand miles away, a simple solution. It took eighteen hundred years to eradicate slavery from the economic structure, and it has to be done again and again in other forms. We cannot assume that we have eighteen hundred years to abolish the colour bar. We shall be lucky if we have eighty, or eighteen; and any suggestion that 'anyhow it will last my time' is intrinsically damnable and politically suicidal.

But the political complexity cannot be allowed to obscure the fact that the moral issue for the Christian is absolutely simple. To translate the new thing in Christ into representation and franchise and trade union rules involves countless technical and social factors, on which Christians will quite properly be divided. But on the basic issue and direction Christians cannot have two minds. This question of racial unity is, I believe, the acid test of Christianity in our century. If we were true to the New Testament and had the courage and accepted the consequences of our convictions, the scandal of the quotation from which I started could never arise.

'Ee! Monare—that is the religion for us Africans'—and for us Europeans and Asiatics. The very possibility of evangelism, of there being a gospel to preach, is involved. It is either the one, corporate Christ, the *totus Christus*, or there is literally nothing.

# CHAPTER TEN

# The Gospel and Health[1]

But if it is by the finger of God that I cast out demons,
then the kingdom of God has come upon you (*Luke 11. 20*).

TOWARDS THE END of last year I received a letter from your
Chaplain at the Guild of Health, Dr Michael Wilson. He enclosed
an article on 'Sickness, Healing and the Will of God' by Dr
Ramsey, the Archbishop of York,[2] and asked me on behalf of
the Executive whether I would reply to it. I am afraid I had to
write back and say that I found myself in almost complete
agreement with the Archbishop, and added, for good value, that
I thought he had put his finger on a number of points where I
had long been uneasy about the theology of the Guild of Health!
I felt I knew Dr Wilson well enough to know that he would not
take offence at this friendly riposte. But I confess I was surprised
when the next communication I received was the invitation to
preach at this annual service. It was heaping coals of fire indeed—
and perhaps I may use this very gracious opportunity, as it may
have been intended that I should, for the somewhat more ex-
tended study of the theological issues to which he also urged me
in his letter.

But I do not forget that this is a sermon, a preaching and
exposition of the Gospel. And it is with the Gospel that I should
like to begin, and to end. For all that I want to say comes out
of it.

The Gospel is the gospel or good news of the Kingdom, of the
reign of God breaking into, transforming and renewing this
world-order of sin, decay and death. The New Testament makes

[1] A Sermon preached at the annual service of *The Guild of Health* in St
Martin-in-the-Fields, London, October 2, 1958.

[2] *The York Quarterly*, November 1957.

it quite plain that this transformation is total in its scope. There is no level of human existence, and indeed no level of natural and cosmic existence, that is not affected by the act of God in Christ and upon which its redemptive and restorative power has not to be brought to bear. Alike in the 'signs' which mark its invasion in the ministry of Jesus and in the end-picture of a new heaven and a new earth, it is clear that matter as well as spirit, disease as well as sin, comes under its sentence of radical and glorious renewal. There is no preaching of the Gospel consistent with the New Testament which does not include the charge 'Heal the sick': without that it would simply be a different gospel. I need not labour that in these circles. I emphasize it because I believe that the recovery of this aspect of our Faith, in a manner that is fully integrated both with the wholeness of the Gospel and with the wholeness of the Church, is one of the most important unfinished tasks of our generation, in which the Guild of Health has played a most honourable part.

Indeed, it is precisely because I believe the matter is so important and the part of this Guild so decisive that I am jealous, as a student of the New Testament, for our perspective to be right.

Let me then return to the New Testament, to the text from which I started: 'If it is by the finger of God that I cast out demons, then the kingdom of God has come upon you'. From these words I should like to draw two simple points.

The first is that health and the giving of health is for the New Testament always a sign of the Kingdom, a pointer to its presence and power. The Gospel is the gospel of the Kingdom; it is not the gospel of health. Jesus heals because, being what he is, the bearer of God's reign of love, he can do no other: not to heal would be to proclaim some other gospel, some other God. And the power by which he heals, as the Beelzebub controversy from which the words are taken makes clear, is an unmistakable indication, for those who have the eyes to see it, of what has been released in their midst. To John the Baptist too the healing works of Christ are given as the most notable sign of the dawning of the new age. But it is the Kingdom, not health, that Jesus has come to bring. He did not come primarily to abolish disease. As Dr Ramsey said in his article, 'We notice scenes where Christ deliberately avoids the crowds who come to him for healing. He healed—for his compassion overflowed: but we are not told that he sought the sick as he sought sinners'. We may not simply ignore these facts. God's will for men is indeed health rather than sickness, life rather than death: Jesus shows us that beyond doubt. Yet healing was for him but one sign of the Kingdom, and towards the end of his ministry, apparently, one of decreasing prominence. How do we account for this? It is not enough to say that he had more important things upon which to concentrate. Why were they more important? If we are not careful, we soon find ourselves saying they were more important to him because they were more 'spiritual'—and that I am sure is a fundamental distortion of the Gospel. The reason, rather, is to be sought in the second fact that emerges from our text.

Jesus claims that in his acts of healing the kingdom of God has 'come upon' or overtaken those he is addressing—and the Greek word contains within it the idea of something that has come before its time. Usually indeed he speaks of the Kingdom as merely having 'drawn near'. The perfect reign of God is of its nature something that belongs to 'the age to come'; but in his ministry it breaks through into this age, penetrating it with the shafts of another order, as the rays of the sun light up the sky before its rising. With the Resurrection we may say that the sun rises, but it shines still upon an old world where sin and disease and death have not yet been done away.

It is most important to remember that this is the perspective in which the whole of the New Testament's teaching on health is set. It is indeed God's will that death shall be done away, that mourning and crying and pain shall be no more. But it is quite evidently not God's will that death shall be done away within this age. Even those whom Jesus raises from the dead have to die again—and they must die of something. Jesus shows that he is even now the resurrection and the life—for body as well as for soul—as he is even now the healer of all our diseases. But he does not go around raising men from the dead for its own sake or even for their sakes. We might be bold to say that he does Lazarus no good by raising him from the dead, except in so far as Lazarus, like the disciples, comes through it to 'see the glory of God'. Jesus *saves* him from nothing, not even perhaps from a more horrible death.

That we die, within this age, is one of the most certain and God-ordained facts in the New Testament: for flesh and blood cannot inherit the kingdom of God. What we die of, and when we die, depends a very great deal on human ignorance, carelessness and sin; and if we are not committed to fighting this ignorance, carelessness and sin at every level and by every means we are not committed to the Gospel. But the Gospel nowhere commits us to believing that sickness and death will disappear within this age; it gives 'no warrant at all', as the Archbishop of York said, 'for the notion that if only the Church's faith were as it should be, disease would everywhere yield to its ministrations'. We cannot say that if healing does not take place, it is simply because we have not enough faith. That was not what God told St Paul when he prayed three times that his 'thorn in the flesh' should be removed and it was not. His answer was rather: 'My grace is sufficient for you'.

What we offer men in healing, when we offer them the Gospel, is in its fullest and richest sense 'the grace of God'. That grace is certainly not merely food for the soul. And yet it is given, like the sacrament which mediates it, to preserve both body and soul 'unto everlasting life'. It is not given in the first instance to preserve what St Paul calls 'the life that I live in the flesh'. It may indeed do that; for the life of 'the body', of a man's entire personality, is so interconnected at every level. And if it does do so, it is a 'sign', like the healing and raising miracles of the Gospels, of that resurrection of the body which is God's destiny for the whole universe. But the Gospel does not stand or fall by whether that sign is given, any more than it did for the thousands whom Jesus did not heal or than it did for St Paul when God made it plain to him that it was not his will for his weakness to be removed.

We should, I believe, be very careful about what we promise people and how we speak of the will of God in this matter. Of course, health is the will of God and disease is the work of the devil: we may never say that sickness is *sent* by God. Death is the last enemy. Yet, by that very token, it is part of God's design that it should be allowed to operate and to reap its harvest *until* the End. It is only then that death shall be no more—and with it the whole process of decay to which the outward man is subject. This is part of the will of God—and that means part of the will of God for individuals—not in the sense that he wills them to suffer, but in the sense that his strength is, within this age, made perfect only out of weakness—the weakness and mortality that inevitably belongs to 'the flesh'. Of course, we must say there are no such things as incurable diseases: God can and may cure anything. But not even of the man closest to Jesus was it promised that he should not die. And of some, particularly of old people whose strength and faculties are exhausted, we may surely say that it is God's will that they should die, that, as the saying goes, he should 'take them' rather than restore them to another few months' useless pain or senility.

'*Nevertheless*'—in all this decay—'know this, that the kingdom of God has drawn near'. And the healing works of Jesus and his raisings from the dead proclaim in dramatic fashion that kingdom's power and the quality of the life it offers. It is the life that 'overcomes the world', with all its sin and sordidness and suffering. That is the life we have to preach, the life that knows no ending, that acknowledges no barriers in the realm of spirit or of matter. And we preach it most signally when we continue Jesus' commission to heal the sick and bring to this faithless world the power of the Prince of Life. But let it be the full gospel of the Kingdom that we offer and not one which, by claiming to set no limits to the will of God or to the power of faith, takes that offer out of the time within which the New Testament places it, the time, that is, *between* the Resurrection and the promised Day of the Lord with its end to pain, disease and death. We cannot offer that Day as a present reality to any individual without qualification.

Till that Day, even we who have the first fruits of the Spirit are not exempt from the groanings and the sufferings of this present time. Yet in them all we have the certain hope that the whole creation shall be set free from its bondage to decay, to enter upon the glorious liberty of the children of God. And still the most manifest sign of that final redemption of our bodies is the Spirit's power to heal. It is indeed but an anticipation, vouchsafed mysteriously and graciously to some, withheld equally mysteriously and graciously from others; and it should not be offered as more. Nevertheless, to us, as to Jesus, *are* given the powers of the age to come; and we may, indeed we must, say to men: 'If we by the finger of God cast out demons, then the kingdom of God has come upon you!'

In discussion provoked by this address the question was raised whether the Christian ideal was not even now a perfect wholeness of body, mind and spirit, with death coming simply as the transition from one level of existence to another, unaccompanied by disease or pain.

This is doubtless the kind of ideal we have in mind when we pray, for instance, for 'a quiet night and *a perfect end*'. The question remains, however, whether the New Testament holds out any promise of its fulfilment. The nearest approximation to such a conception is in I Thess. 5.23: 'May the God of peace himself sanctify you wholly; and may your spirit and soul and body be kept sound and blameless at the coming of our Lord Jesus Christ'. This certainly gives warrant for the *direction* in which all healing activity must tend. God is the God of peace, and his ideal for man is a 'wholeness' in which nothing is lost, nothing unreconciled, nothing unsanctified. But it is equally clear that this is an ultimate ideal: it is what St Paul prays will be true for the Thessalonians at the coming of Christ, which, it should be remembered he is expecting in this Epistle to overtake the majority, including himself, *before* they have to face the dissolution of death.

He is indeed convinced that the incidence of death can make no difference to whether or not a man attains the Christian goal (I Thess. 4.13-18). All will be 'changed' (I Cor. 15.52) so radically that those who have not died will enjoy no advantage (I Thess. 4.15). Nevertheless, the Apostle's own preference is clearly that what is mortal should be swallowed up into life *without his having to be 'unclothed'* (II. Cor. 5.4). The ideal transition from one order of existence to another is not a perfect death (a combination of words we cannot imagine on his lips) but one that avoids death altogether. Death for him remains abhorrent and diabolic. God in Christ has, to be sure, drawn its sting and given us the victory over it (I Cor. 15.54-7). Yet the great paean of praise which rounds off his chapter on the resurrection is introduced by the phrase: 'When the perishable puts on the imperishable, and the mortal puts on immortality, *then* shall come to pass the saying that is written: "Death is swallowed up in victory" '. And this moment occurs, as he has just insisted, only at the last trump (I Cor. 15.52). St Paul holds out no hope that any transition before that, and therefore any transition that includes death, will be anything but painful and destructive. Such a transition may indeed be abundantly worth it: for the Christian to die is actually 'gain' (Phil. 1.21-3). But nothing can make the process of dying anything but the end term of that 'decay', 'enmity' and 'wrath' to which man and creation are at present subject.

Wholeness, the perfect reflection of 'the God of peace', does not belong to man within this age, by virtue of his creation. He is indeed made in the image of God, but that image is blurred and jarred and broken by sin. Christ alone is the perfect image of God, 'the proper man'. 'The complete man' (Eph. 4.13) is the *Totus Christus*, which, short of the final redintegration of humanity in the body of his glory, remains unattained. Perfect wholeness of body, mind and spirit is not an ideal which is held out in the New Testament either for immediate or for individual attainment. Health, salvation, is essentially both corporate and ultimate. Meanwhile, in the new life of the Body of Christ, the healing community, there is offered the pledge and anticipation of that resurrection of the body which is God's destiny for all creation. The Church *is* indeed the resurrection Body of Christ within history, by incorporation into which mankind is given even now the victory over the alienation, disease and disintegration that afflict God's racked creation. But there is no promise that 'the powers', 'the world-rulers of this darkness', to whose activity all this is attributed, will finally be 'destroyed' short of the End (I Cor. 15.24-6). A perfect death, physically as well as spiritually, is something that we may feel that we do occasionally see, as a glimpse, an anticipation, of the time when 'death shall be no more, neither shall there be mourning nor crying nor pain any more'. But we cannot promise it as part of the Gospel to men and women within this age. For the condition of that promise has not been fulfilled: 'the former things' have not yet 'passed away' (Rev. 21.4).

CHAPTER ELEVEN

# Preaching Death[1]

ONE OF THE PENALTIES of writing on the Last Things is that you find yourself becoming a sort of theological mortician. If anyone wants death brought up to date they say, 'Oh, send for John Robinson'. I really don't fancy myself in this macabre profession. In fact, I want to play death down rather than play it up. In one sense, of course, we don't think of it anything like enough. Indeed, the whole of American civilization could almost be said to be constructed with the object of evading what the Revised Standard Version so delicately calls, in the Lazarus story, the 'odor' of death. A little more healthy *memento mori* would not do any of us any harm.

But having said that, I want also to say the opposite, namely, that the whole of our Western tradition has contrived to give death an altogether inflated significance. There has been a vastly exaggerated focus on death and the moment of death. It began when the pages of the New Testament were hardly dry, and it is one of the most remarkable silent revolutions in the history of Christian thought.

Let me remind you of three ways in which you have been brought up to think of death—unless, that is, you happen to be the son of a biblical theologian born since about 1945.

(1) The whole of our teaching and our hymnology has assumed that you go to heaven—or, of course, hell—when you die.

(2) In consequence, death is the decisive moment. Though you may go on after that, on one road or the other, it is your life up till then that determines your destiny.

[1] The substance of a sermon preached to an undergraduate congregation at the University Church of St Mary-the-Virgin, Oxford, on March 8, 1959.

E

(3) We do not, of course, these days believe in anything so crude as the resurrection of the body; but, if there is to be any other form of existence, it is at death that we enter it.

Now I believe that each of these three propositions is in clear contradiction with what the Bible says, and that together they give death, and the moment of death, an importance to which it has no right in the Christian scheme.

(1) First, the Bible nowhere says that we go to heaven when we die, nor does it ever describe death in terms of going to heaven. In the Old Testament, you went to *sheol* when you died (the only people who went to heaven were those like Enoch and Elijah who never died). In the New Testament, our destiny as Christians is indeed to be with Christ in the heavenly places. But that is nowhere because we die, but (*a*) because we are baptized, and (*b*) *despite* the fact that in the interval we may die, because Christ will include in his final triumph those who by their union with him are already risen men. Death for the New Testament is of great significance for the 'old man' (which of course means for most of us most of the time): it is the sacrament and seal of sin, the last term of that stripping down which leaves us exposed and naked before him with whom we have to do. But death has no crucial significance in the calendar of the new life. Here the only relevant moments are Baptism and the *Parousia*.

(2) The second assumption, that death is the decisive moment for our eternal destiny (whether we are actually judged then or, as it were, held in cold storage for judgement at the last day) is one that has been deeply ingrained in both Catholic and Protestant thought. Indeed, St Thomas Aquinas wrote it into his system to the extent of saying that, since only matter and that which was in matter could change, a man's condition after death was strictly unalterable. Death, as it were, was what 'fixed' him—even though the dross might still have to be purged away. Hence the horror of dying in mortal sin and the dread of sudden, and therefore unprepared, death for which we still pray to be delivered in the Litany. And traditional Protestant thought, in reaction against 'the Popish doctrine of purgatory', has gone even further and held that at death a man passes beyond the need even of purgation

or prayer. If he is among the elect he is at once made fit for communion with Christ; if he is not, he is out.

Now, few people, I suspect, really believe this today. And yet the decisiveness of the place which death occupies in our thinking is unabated. If you are an Evangelical, saving a man before he dies, or, if you are a Catholic, baptizing him before he dies, is still a 'must'. But the Bible never says that a man must be brought to Christ before he dies, or else . . . On the one hand, it says, 'Now is the day of salvation—while it is called today.' On the other hand, it says that God has the ages of ages in which to work and wills all men to be saved and to come to the knowledge of the truth. The idea that God is finished unless one of his ministers can get me before the next bus runs me down in the High is blasphemy. 'Death, where is thy victory?' On this reckoning, it would seem, over ninety in every hundred. One would hardly think that Christ had cast death from its throne if this were the limit it can still impose upon the saving work of God.

(3) This notion that a man's destiny is decided at death is one for which there is no real support in the biblical imagery.[1] It is in the Greek mythology that the fates operate at death with their scissors and scales. The reason why it seems natural to us as Christians is that we have come to regard judgement, as in the West we have come to regard persons, purely atomistically. Each man's ledger, as it were, is totted up independently when his account closes. And precisely the same applies to our thinking, if any, on the third point, the resurrection of the body. The resurrection body is pictured as a sort of new suit, tailor-made for us to put on the moment we set foot on 'the other side'. Observe once more the influence of the classical mythology in the Charon myth: the baptizing of it in Wesley's words 'Bid Jordan's narrow stream divide, and bring us safe to heaven' has no biblical basis. Indeed, it would be interesting to know at what stage the Styx first became the Jordan.

[1] Heb. 9.27, 'It is appointed for men to die once, and after that comes judgement' is often quoted to the contrary. But with the rest of the New Testament the Author to the Hebrews associates the Judgement with the *Parousia*, with which indeed it stands parallel in this passage.

The idea that we put on the resurrection body at death is again without scriptural foundation (though II Cor. 5.1—'we have a house not made with hands, eternal in the heavens', has sometimes been made to say this in the face of every other indication in the New Testament). Rather, according to the New Testament, we put on the new man (a) at Baptism, when we are incorporated into the resurrection body of Christ, and (b) finally, at the consummation of God's plan, when the redemption of our body, the transformation of this order of existence into the new world of God's creation, will stand forth complete.

Meanwhile, though our outward man is decaying (despite death, that is, not in any sense because of it), our inward man, our new solidarity in the body of Christ, is being built up day by day. The resurrection of the body, like Christianity itself, is something social; it is 'put on' as we are brought into Christ and built up into his body. That is why the resurrection of the body is always associated in the New Testament with the *Totus Christus*, the Complete Man, the revelation of Jesus Christ with all his saints. Like salvation (with which indeed the redemption of the body is virtually equated in Romans 8), it cannot be complete for any till it is complete for all.

I have spent a good deal of time clearing away undergrowth. But let me end by trying to state the heart of the Christian hope, as succinctly and as positively as I can. And I will do it from a text which, typically, does not mention death at all. It comes from the third chapter of the Epistle to the Philippians, vv.20 and 21: 'Our commonwealth is in heaven, and from it we await a Saviour, the Lord Jesus Christ, who will change our lowly body to be like his glorious body, by the power which enables him even to subject all things to himself.'

From this text notice briefly three things.

(1) First, our commonwealth or citizenship is in heaven. Whatever else that means, it means that heaven is where we already belong. 'Passports for heaven' is a phrase which sums up one whole way of thinking about Christianity. But if the Christian holds a passport, it is not a passport to get him to heaven (at death), but a passport from heaven to live within this world as

the representative and ambassador of a foreign style of life. In Moffatt's inspired rendering, the Church's function is to be a colony of heaven—because its members are already by baptism citizens of heaven. If they only became so as they migrated from this world they would be a lot of good in this world!

(2) The second point is that the Christian hope is not so much a hope for heaven as a hope from heaven: for 'from it we await a Saviour, the Lord Jesus Christ'. The heart of the Christian hope is not that the housing committee of the celestial city council will one day move us from this slum to that 'other country' of Cecil Spring-Rice's hymn, 'whose shining bounds increase' as 'soul by soul and silently' death transfers from earth to heaven those who are on its list. The heart of the Christian hope is rather that the life of God (heaven) will so penetrate the life of man (earth) that God's will shall be done on earth as it is in heaven. Of that movement from God to man the Incarnation is the pledge, the *Parousia* is the promise. For with the complete coming of Christ into everything, there is promised that new heaven and new earth which, as the Seer saw, must also come down out of heaven from God.

(3) But, thirdly, what is the relation of the new to the old? This is the crucial point for our attitude to all the things of this world—to politics, economics and everything else. And, contrary to what is usually supposed, this is where the resurrection of the body comes in—not with death but with drains. According to a dominant, if not the dominant, Christian tradition, the world is regarded as a vast transit camp, in which the Church's job is to issue tickets for heaven and pack people off to paradise, leaving this old collection of Nissen huts to tumble to decay. But according to the Christian gospel God has prepared some better thing for the work of his hands. The gospel of the reign of God is not the salvaging of souls from a mass of perdition, but 'the redemption of the body', that is, the redintegration of the whole man in all his relationships, physical and spiritual, in a new solidarity which creates personality rather than destroys it. And the gospel goes on to insist that this new man has already been created, in the body of Christ, and that within the life of the

Church the new God-given structure of existence has even now begun to penetrate and transform this world. Into that new structure of existence the whole body of our present life is ultimately to be taken up and conformed to his glorious body, 'by the power which enables him even to subject all things to himself'.

Such is the Christian's goal, the new world order, of which within this world he is the ambassador and the agent. And he will no more think it irrelevant to his life here than the Communist will lose sight of his ideal and (as he believes) coming society. What *is* irrelevant is that particular breaking point in the old order which we call death, and the pagan notion, endorsed by so much Christian spirituality, that life is the preparation for death. Concentration on that is what really takes the Christian's eye off the ball and makes him spiritually self-centred and politically futile. As if for risen men whose real death is behind them, the moment of physical death can any longer be the focus of their gaze! Our gaze as Christians is not at death, nor even beyond it at the skies, but at God's world from the other side of it. And from there, where Christ is seated at the right hand of God, 'O death, where is thy victory? O grave, where is thy sting?'

# CHAPTER TWELVE

# Preaching Judgement[1]

DURING HIS MISSION to London, I took a non-Christian friend to hear Billy Graham. He preached that night on the text: 'And after that the judgement.' Afterwards, my friend, a highly intelligent research mathematician, said: 'Tell me, what do you mean by judgement? I don't understand.'

That struck me as a significant remark. For the first time for centuries we are living in a world where men have no idea what judgement means. Until recently the traditional picture of a day of judgement still bounded men's horizons. If it meant nothing else, it gave them the sense that at the last frontier there was a customs to face. As recently as Kipling, Judgement Day comes into the most secular literature in a perfectly natural way.

Moreover, the idea of judgement is not a specifically Christian one. It is noticeable how St Paul, always a speaker acutely alive to his audience, seized upon it as one of his few points of contact in a wholly pagan setting. An appeal to creation, to conscience, and to the fact of judgement—these were the themes in his gospel to 'the outsider', as he preached it at Athens, and as he reproduces it in the Epistle to the Romans. Later, before the pagan governor Felix, we are told that he commended the faith of Christ by 'arguing about justice and self-discipline and judgement to come'. And Felix at any rate understood sufficiently to adjourn the hearing in evident discomfort.

But today we live in a world of justice without judgement. Our moral sense, if not our morality, is strong, and, Christian and humanist alike, we draw up our charters of human rights. But judgement is an embarrassing theme. It looks as though we believed in rights, but would be alarmed to have them vindicated.

Perhaps we have ceased to believe in judgement in heaven

[1] Reprinted from *The Preacher's Quarterly*, September and December, 1957.

because we have lost any confidence in judgement on earth. When the final arbiter of human affairs is not an international court but the hydrogen bomb, is it surprising that men think of the End not as a consummation, marked by judgement, but as mere cessation, whether with a bang or a whimper?

But let us analyse this notion of judgement more closely, and try to see why it is strange to our age. It contains in its most general form at least three main ideas.

(1) The first is that the universe is not morally neutral, that the world is so built that in the end *right will out*. We should note that this is a conviction not simply about what ought to be, but about what is, about the brute nature of 'things'. It presupposes, in Edward Caird's phrase, that 'what ought to be rests upon a deeper is than what ought not to be'.

Now in different degrees most people in fact cling to some such faith. We believe that somehow a way of life founded upon freedom and truth must in the end prove stronger than one based on fear and lies. We believe that in history we do see judgement overtaking the Napoleons and Hitlers of this world. We believe that a racial policy such as we are watching in South Africa today must bring its own retribution. For a time men may be able to evade the consequences of their actions, but in the long run these catch up on them or their successors.

So we judge, and thereby we confess that the idea of judgement is not wholly foreign to us. But what about the longer run still, when, as it were, the sea finally comes in over the sand-castles of human history? Will the processes of judgement which we think we can trace within history have any further validity? Will not the last word simply be with 'things' and not with persons or personal values at all? In the final analysis, does not our modern age—don't we in so far as we are part of it—believe in a world without judgement? A *last* judgement, which says that the universe itself is not neutral—that takes too much believing.

(2) The second idea contained in judgement is that of division, of a final separation between sheep and goats. But in a world where we are used to seeing all things as relative—our hopes, our standards, even our science—any ultimate division into black and

white strikes us as intolerable. Everything within us—our charity as well as our cynicism—conspires to tell us that we are all going the same way. And it is notable that one of the most characteristic marks of Spiritualism—the only current creed of a life after death to awaken a flicker of response—is that it contains no idea of judgement. Its great attraction is that it offers going on in the grey, without having to face the awful prospect of white or black.

(3) The third element in judgement is the simple but disturbing thought that we have a judge, someone else standing over us. We can get along with the idea that we judge ourselves, by what we are and what we do. For that comes to much the same as saying there is no judgement; we simply find our own level, as we do in the social scale. But the idea of a judge standing over us, of some-one *else* to whom we must render account—that sets up more resistance than any other article in the Christian Creed. For it reminds us that we are finite and that we are guilty at the same time: it is not agreeable.

All these three elements—that the universe is not morally neutral, that we are not all going the same way, that we are not our own judges—have combined to make modern man reject the idea of judgement. We live, in this twentieth century, in a world without judgement, a world where at the last frontier post you simply go out—and nothing happens. It is like coming to the customs and finding there are none after all. And the suspicion that this is in fact the case spreads fast: for it is what we should all *like* to believe.

And yet in face of this the Christian gospel still has the naïvety to declare that 'God has fixed a day on which he will judge the world in righteousness by a man whom he has appointed'.

The day of judgement! How vivid a picture that evoked in the minds of our forefathers! They lived with it on their walls, and it filled their west windows; it played on their imaginations and seared their consciences. Yet today that picture lies gathering dust in the attic of our minds. We have all of us a recollection of it, maybe a keen and terrible recollection, of some vast tribunal at the end of the world where God is seated on a great white throne and the books are opened and every word and every action that anyone has ever said or done is brought out as evidence against him. It seems to our generation a bizarre scene—and utterly remote. Doomsday! The very word is a symbol for the farthest remove of time, when everything else is over. And if we are asked what we ourselves really think about the day of judgement, is not the honest answer that we don't think about it?

Now if we want to restore any contact between our world and the idea of judgement, I suggest that we begin by leaving that picture where it is—up in the attic. Later we may find ourselves returning to it and seeing more in it than we thought. But to our world its associations are with the fantastic and the remote, and with a great deal that is frankly sub-Christian; and if we start trying to do our re-thinking within its frame, we shall lose touch with reality at once.

Let us start with the most fundamental idea of all which the Christian gospel has to set against the basic suspicion of our modern world. It is, at its absolute simplest, that when we go out we encounter, not nothing, but *God*. Everything we are and everything we do does not run out into emptiness: it runs up into him, into his love and his holiness. He is the frontier by which all our life is bounded. And he is the frontier also by which the whole of history is bounded: it too does not go out into nothingness; it runs up into him. That is the significance of a judgement set where the Bible sets it, not merely at the close of every individual life, but at the end of the world. It is saying that the whole process of the universe also 'adds up', and that none of our lives can be judged by themselves alone, but only in relation to this final account.

Now this idea that the whole of history 'adds up', that you must speak of a reckoning here too, is in fact something we owe almost wholly to the Bible. We have so grown up with the conception of a last judgement that we tend to forget that all men everywhere have not shared it. But while the ancient Greeks, for instance, pictured each man's life being weighed in the balance at death, they never thought of the whole process of history leading up to anything: it just went round in a circle, like nature.

But while the vision of a *last* judgement is the great contribution of the Old Testament—and it is to this that we owe ultimately all idea of progress, of history 'getting somewhere'—it is not the only or the most important thing the Bible has to say about judgement. For the New Testament introduces a fresh theme, which is still so unfamiliar that one cannot even state it without sounding para-doxical. It is that the last judgement has already happened.

That, of course, is absurd. To see what it means we may go back once more to our basic conception of judgement as encountering God. A *last* judgement means to be 'up against it' once and for all, or rather to be up against him once and for all, in such a way that there is simply nothing more to be said. Now the message of the New Testament is that we have no need to wait to the end of history, or even the end of our lives, to be up against God's last word. For in Jesus Christ we meet him in such a way that there is nothing more for him to say. Instead of waiting for us to meet him, whether at the frontier of death or at the end of the world, he has come over the frontier, into history, to meet us. That is why the New Testament regularly speaks of God *coming* to judge the world.

With the coming of Jesus Christ the last judgement is on. For men's response to Jesus *is* their response to God: 'He who denies me before men will be denied before the angels of God'. In Jesus and his claim we are up against God in a way that can never be more final. It is no longer a case of waiting to see what God's judgement will be. For 'now is the day of salvation'; and that means 'now is the day of judgement'. Jesus cannot be the light of the world without being also its judge. Indeed, 'this *is* the judge-ment, that the light has come into the world and men loved darkness rather than light'.

What then has become of the day of judgement? Does it mean that it is all now past and finished with? Has it rightly dropped out of our present-day Christianity? No; as I shall insist in a moment. Yet, to be true to the gospel, we must stress, more than perhaps we have, the deep sense in which this world has been judged already once and for all. 'Now is the judgement of this world,' said Jesus at the moment of his passion, and he assured his disciples that the Spirit would convict the world in this matter of judgement 'because the prince of this world has been judged'. That is to say, the Spirit is to bring home the fact that the death of Jesus *was* the final indictment of this world. Ever since it has been a world with a cross in it. Now, after Calvary, we know just what man is like and just what God is like. The final issues of life and death have been revealed. From that moment onwards the history of the world is the judgement of the world, lived out under the sign of the Son of man, as it comes to terms with him.

We have been judged, this world of ours, finally. And we are being judged, as we crucify the Son of God afresh or as we let that love break and convict us. What is certain is that there is nothing *else* by which we shall be judged. Yet if the day of judgement is on, it is not over. For judgement means the justification of God, the manifest and final vindication of love's design. And God is not finished till that is accomplished—till he is all in all. There *is* a consummation of his purpose for the entire universe, a summing up of all things in Christ. Nothing the New Testament has to say here goes back on the Old. But what it does say is that this day of judgement is not simply future, as it was for the Jews. And certainly it is not remote. For he whom we shall confront is he who has already met us in Jesus Christ, and who meets us now at every moment of our living.

'God with us', Emmanuel: that is the Christmas message for which Advent prepares us. It does so by reminding us that this is a very solemn as well as a very joyful fact. God comes into the human family—to stay. Now having someone in your house who comes to stay and never goes is a sobering prospect. It means adjusting yourself to going on living with him for ever. And that is no light thing, especially if he is a person you once tried to murder. For the rest of your days there is no getting away from him: everything you do hits him and everything he does hits you. It is something like this that the Christian means by saying that we are living already in the day of judgement. As a human family, in our most intimate lives, we have One living with us who at every moment convicts us by his goodness, his unselfishness, his endless bearing of our rebuffs. And a judgement like that is certainly nothing remote! It is all too oppressively close.

And yet, let us be honest, most of the time it does not feel like this. If it did it would be intolerable; the judgement of it would simply stifle us. Every now and then, to be sure, we may suddenly realize that what we have just done—the lie we have told, the cruel word, the evil thought that has filled our mind—has fallen upon his ears, his love, his purity; and then something snaps, and we begin to know what Peter must have felt when in the moment of denial the Lord turned and looked upon him. At such an hour the cock-crow can go through us like the last trump. For a flash we sense what judgement really means, and what it is like never to be met by anything less than endless love.

But it is not always, or often thus. Much more frequently we are conscious of no judgement at all, and we find ourselves saying, 'Lord, we never knew . . . When did we see thee hungry or thirsty or a stranger?' And this brings me to the last thing I want to say about the Christian idea of judgement. What is distinctive in Christianity is not merely the idea, revolutionary as it is, that the last judgement has already begun. It consists also in the prin-ciple, introduced with Jesus Christ, by which this judgement operates. While Judaism was content to say simply that God would judge the world by his own righteousness, Christianity sees the judgement, like the salvation, of God mediated through *a man* and communicated under the form of a servant. And this insight finds its classic expression in the passage from which I have just quoted, the vision of the Last Judgement embodied in the so-called parable of the Sheep and the Goats.

'When did we see thee hungry, or thirsty, or a stranger . . . '? The plain fact is that they hadn't. All the time that they were being judged, and judged finally, they had never seen him on whom their actions fell. The New Testament insists that Christ *comes* to be our judge—he comes over the frontier to meet us. Yet equally we could say that he judges us by removing himself. 'It is expedient for you', he said, 'that I go away'. In his mercy he judges us in this world not by confronting us with himself but by confronting us with our neighbour. The divine judgement, unless it is to blind us like the lightning flash, must always come to us *incognito*. That was the pattern in the days of Christ's flesh. He came among men as one whom they met, not as God, but as their neighbour, as one of themselves. In flashes of faith they apprehended in that neighbour him by whom they were really being convicted. But if it had not been for the remove at which God stood, that conviction would not have dawned as a moral judgement, coming from the inside, passed on themselves by themselves. It would simply have overwhelmed them from without.

And so it is with the Christ of glory: he too, within this present life, must come to us *incognito*. There are moments, as it were of transfiguration, when, in the day to day encounter with our neighbour, the cloud breaks and the vision comes over us of the Christ by whom truly we are met. It is in some such glimpses that our *sense* of judgement is most vivid. But it is not only in such moments that we are being judged, any more than it was only at the Transfiguration that Jesus was judging his generation. For most of them, most even of his own followers, had no such vision. And so it is today. To say that 'now is the day of judgement' is not to say that the judgement is there to be seen. For at present the process is a hidden one: it is the period when the wheat grows together with the tares. The New Testament indeed looks beyond to what it calls 'the revealing of the Son of man', the moment of unveiling when he meets us no longer as *a* son of man, but as *the* Son of man, as the King he is. That is the moment of which the parable of the Sheep and the Goats is speaking. But it is not this moment alone which is there seen as the day of judgement. This moment in fact merely reveals that the judgement is already over: it exposes him by whom all along, without knowing it, they *have been* judged.

Yet the form of the servant is no mere disguise, like the prince in the fairy story dressed as a beggar. It is of the essence of the Christian gospel that the agent of judgement should be the Son of man, the One who is himself the true Man. For in confronting us with himself, Christ confronts us with nothing alien to ourselves. He confronts us with our own humanity. He comes to meet us in the neighbour, in the one whose sole claim upon us is simply that he is man—in the starving, the destitute, the suffering. Christ wills to judge us through them, to let them be our judges.

I spoke earlier of judgement in terms of having to live with God for ever. Yet for our judging we are called to live not with the naked holiness of him who is of purer eyes than to behold iniquity; not even with the intolerable judgement of a perfect man; but simply with the pensioner next door. 'Art thou neighbour?' 'How much have you loved?' It is not necessary, as the hymn says, to 'soar through tracts unknown' to see him on his judgement throne. For he is very nigh, looking at us out of the eyes of our fellow man.

The Son of man is to be our judge. In that lies a knowledge that casts out fear, the fear of the unknown, a terror of the absolute remoteness with which the day of judgement has so often been clothed. For it is by the image of God—in others, in ourselves, in the One who is himself the very image of the invisible God—that we are to be judged. To be judged is in fact to come home, to come to ourselves, as we were made by God to be. This is indeed a truly shattering thing: for it is to be confronted with the picture also of what we have made ourselves. But it is, nevertheless, to come home, to a Father and to a family from which, however distantly, we have gone out. It is to come home to live with that family, to live with ourselves, to live with him. It is in every sense 'our own place' to which we go, even if we have made it our own hell.

Such is the principle of judgement in Jesus Christ. From that it would be natural to go on to ask, What is the end of judgement? Is it indeed possible that God, the Father of our Lord Jesus Christ, should *for ever* be content for any to live with him and find it hell? For myself, I cannot think so, if we really believe in his almightiness *as love*. But to do justice to the problems which this raises is impossible in the space that is left.[1] What we can say, and must, is that to speak of judgement alone is not to declare the whole counsel of God, for 'God did not send his Son into the world to judge the world, but that the whole world through him might be saved'.

The concern which has governed my choice of theme has been how we may make our *preaching* of judgement more effective. What scenes of power that phrase calls up! And how weak and flickering our occasional excursions into this 'appendix' of Christian doctrine! We know we must speak on it from time to time, but there is no fire in our bellies. We haven't the stomach to give

[1] I have tried to give what answer I can to them in the last two chapters of my book *In the End*, *God* . . .

them hell, and even if we try to, it's academic stuff—peripheral, apologetic, and unrelated to men where they are.

One reason certainly, is that the whole Christian myth has at this point lost its power, either to terrify or to move. More than that, it has become a positive obstacle to our generation entertaining the very notion of judgement. There is no point in the Christian Creed at which the case for Dr Bultmann's remedy is so compelling. We must 'demythologize' the Day of Judgement if we are to begin to commend it as a category of relevance to our world. And that indeed is what we have been trying to do.

But when we have done it we have merely removed the obstacle: we have not restored the power. The latter is indeed something we cannot command: it is the work of the Spirit. But we can do something to prepare the channels for its flowing.

If we ask what in our day these will be, we must, I suspect, be prepared for a reappraisal, or rather a revolution, that goes deeper than anything involved in recasting the myth. Here, as elsewhere, what is required of us is above all to reincarnate the truth which the myth was created to preserve. As Dr George Macleod has insisted in his prophetic book, *Only One Way Left*, the real trouble is not with the myth (though it is probably more trouble here than almost anywhere else) but with 'the vacuity we have created at the centre of the myth'. 'Bultmann,' he writes, 'started on his quest (and bless him for every risk he takes) because German soldiers passed by the offer of the Message. But what made them, and modern man, pass by is not the obstacle of mythological concepts: but our *dehumanizing of him who is our sole salvation*'.[1] We have allowed ourselves to forget that the truth of the Last Judgement, as of every other Christian doctrine, is ultimately nothing else but the truth of the Incarnation—namely, that the last Word about God has to be made visible in a Man and through a Man, *and can only so be made visible*. This is not simply the truth about thirty years of history now over and done with; it is the truth about all history. For this Man is upon the throne of God for ever, and this Man is the agent of the final judgement.

The principle of Christian judgement on which we have been

[1] *Op. cit.*, p. 46.

insisting, that it is through man, the Son of man, that the judgement of God comes to us, is thus also, I believe, the clue to the recovery of its power for us. We shall see him on his judgement throne, and behold him coming with power, only as we see him as Man; and that means, as the parable of the Sheep and the Goats makes inescapably clear, only as we see him in man. The myth has lost its power because it has ceased to be earthed. It comes to us as something airborne and remote, no longer rooted, as on the lips of him who spoke it, in the judgement of man by Man in the present encounters of everyday life. The *real* difference between us and the first century is not that we no longer live in a three-decker universe; it is that the Word of judgement is no longer made flesh in our midst.

The corollary of this is that we may expect to encounter the judgement of Christ, as Man and through man, only as, in the biblical phrase, we '*do* judgement', not as we talk about it. And the Church will recover the power to *preach* God's judgement only to the extent that it re-learns its commitment—personal, political, economic—to the least of those through whom the Son of man has chosen to meet us. We speak regularly as though this commitment were a consequence of preaching and receiving the gospel: we should do well to ask ourselves whether it may not also be the condition of our preaching and receiving it. And of no part of the gospel is this more likely to be true than of its word of judgement.

The truth as it is in Jesus is that mankind is ultimately to be judged by its own humanity, by what it really means to be a man. It will understand that truth and accept it only as it *actually finds itself convicted by the Son of man on earth*, that is, by the Church as she takes a towel and girds herself, by her ministers and her members as they 'do judgement' for the least of his brethren. *Then* we may be able once more to *preach* judgement. And what we find ourselves preaching is likely to be much nearer to what the Prophets meant by that word 'judgement' than some of our latter-day evangelists. It will disclose itself, that is to say, not in yet another feverish attempt to fan the flames of hell and make them relevant, so much as in the far more costly proclamation, in deed as well as in word, of the very present judgements of God in the history and society of men where they are.

# CHAPTER THIRTEEN

# Preaching the Second Coming[1]

THE EXHORTATION in the service for the Ordering of Priests, which is one of the finest pieces of English prose in the Book of Common Prayer, contains these words:

> We exhort you, in the name of the Lord Jesus Christ, that you have in remembrance, into how high a dignity, and to how weighty an office and charge ye are called: that is to say, to be messengers, watchmen, and stewards of the Lord.

My task this morning is to pursue a little further what is meant by the calling to be 'watchmen of the Lord' in the world in which we live. For it is as watchmen that our faces are set towards the future, towards the coming of our Lord, whether on the last day or the next day, whether in the consummation of the age or in the signs of the times. 'Watchman, what of the night?' Still the voice comes from Seir (Isa. 21.11), and from every quarter and every area of our racked and puzzled world; and still the world expects that we shall have some answer. How, then, do we preach the gospel at this point, so as to make 'the last things' first things and the future press in upon the present with insistent relevance?

I propose to divide what I have to say into two parts. We will start, first, with the office of the Christian minister as the Lord's watchman, asking ourselves, in the light of the Bible, what it means to be appointed to this charge and whether we know what we are meant to be watching for. And then, secondly, having

[1] A lecture to the Clergy School of the Northern Province at St John's College, York, July 29, 1959.

adjusted our own sights, we may go on to ask what we must preach to others and how we may do it in such a way as to make it relevant and intelligible to them.

I

First, then, let us begin, as we must, from the Bible.

The image of the watchman is one that is deeply rooted in the prophetic tradition. It was Hosea who first said, 'The prophet is the watchman of the people of my God' (Hos. 9. 8), and Isaiah envisaged himself stationed upon a watchtower day and night (Isa. 21.8). Jeremiah sees the leaders of the nation as watchmen set over it by God (Jer. 6.17), and to Ezekiel comes the word: 'Son of man, I have made you a watchman for the house of Israel; whenever you hear a word from my mouth, you shall give them warning from me' (Ezek. 3.17); and with it goes a corresponding responsibility if he fails to give warning. Again in Second Isaiah: 'Upon your walls, O Jerusalem, I have set watchmen; all the day and all the night they shall never be silent.' They are to be 'the Lord's remembrancers', to 'take no rest and give him no rest until he establishes Jerusalem and makes it a praise in the earth' (Isa. 62.6f.). And, like Jeremiah before him, he sees the watchmen as the heralds of the final deliverance of God (Isa. 52.8; Jer. 31.6). But for the watchmen, as for the shepherds, who fail in their duty he has scathing denunciation. 'His watchmen are blind, they are all without knowledge; they are all dumb dogs, they cannot bark; dreaming, lying down, loving to slumber. The dogs have a mighty appetite; they never have enough. The shepherds also have no understanding; they have all turned to their own way, each to his own gain, one and all' (Isa. 56.10f.).

Thus while the shepherd is a symbol for the priestly and pastoral function of the leaders of God's people, the watchman depicts their prophetic task. Their function is to discern and to warn, to pray for and to herald the coming of the Lord to his people.

In the New Testament, the word 'watchman' itself is, rather surprisingly, not to be found. But the verb 'to watch' is constantly reiterated, usually in the imperative. And in the Epistle to the Hebrews, shortly before Jesus himself is designated 'the great shepherd of the sheep', there is a reference to the ministry of the Church which clearly echoes the charge given to Ezekiel: 'Obey your leaders and submit to them; for they are keeping watch over your souls, as men who will have to give account' (Heb. 13.17). And finally, though we do not have the watchman, we have the more pedestrian and less romantic figure of the porter, to whom is given the particular responsibility while the owner is away, to 'be on the watch' (Mark 13.34).

This injunction to watch continues, of course, as the key-note of the Church's Advent season. It is given classic expression in Nicolai's superb hymn, so rich in biblical imagery:

> Wake, O wake, the night is flying!
> The watchmen from the heights are crying.

Yet, if we sing this with gusto and find it, as I do, a constantly fresh thrill, I wonder if it may not be with something of the same zest with which we give ourselves to that other magnificent Advent hymn, 'Lo, he comes with clouds descending', that is to say, in grateful compensation that we can enthuse in song about something which we should be tongue-tied to explain or to expound.

We are ordained as watchmen; yet have we any clear idea what we are watching for? The proper answer, no doubt, is the Second Coming. But what does this mean? What are we really alerting people for? In practice I suspect that the idea of watching has dropped out of our working picture of the ministry. We have vacated the watchtower to Jehovah's Witnesses, and (albeit with a bad conscience) we are quite relieved to let them have it, for we really should not know what to do with it. Let us be honest with ourselves. It is no good simply going on repeating this idea of 'watching' and feeling that it lends an invigorating sense of existential urgency to an otherwise drab routine, if we cannot be more articulate about what we mean by it. What in fact did we visualize to ourselves when, at our ordination as deacons, we heard the words of the Gospel: 'Let your loins be girded about and your lamps burning; and ye yourselves like unto men that wait for their lord' (Luke 12.35f.)? And how did we imagine ourselves waiting for him when we were turned out on to the streets of our parish the next morning?

I propose at this point to spend a short time on some fairly elementary biblical criticism. For one of our main troubles is that on the subject of the last things, in distinction now, at last, from the first things, we have not let our head catch up with our heart. And I am convinced that we shall not be able to teach our people anything really effective about 'watching' till we ourselves have integrated what we have learnt from our New Testament text books with our preaching and pastoralia.

I am sure that most people—and most of us—still think of 'watching for the coming of the Lord' rather, as Fr Gabriel Hebert once described it to me, like waiting for an air-raid. And to suggest that we should be engaged all the time in skinning our eyes like a spiritual observer corps for some cosmic catastrophe that might occur in five seconds time or in five million years is really, as he said, 'a bit steep'. It does not bear any realistic relation to the life we have to live, as priests or as anything else. And the consequence is that the Second Advent drops into the background of the picture as a possibility which we cannot rule out but which we can in practice discount.

Now such a conception of watching is, I believe, a false one, and one that has been shown false time and time again from the Apostolic age onwards. The expectation of an imminent *parousia* on that model in fact proved a dupe and a blind alley. And it is not really very satisfactory simply to retain the same expectation but to go on pushing it further and further off—any more than you meet the problem of the first things intellectually by turning Archbishop Ussher's 4004 B.C. to 4000 million B.C. and leaving everything else the same. A deeper understanding of biblical revelation indicates, surely, that it is just as mistaken to see the *Parousia* as a single datable event of future history as it is to see the Fall as a single datable event of past history. To wait literally for the one to appear in the sky is as wrong-headed as to wait for evidence of the other to be dug up by the archaeologists.

Moreover, I believe that we can say with fair confidence that this sort of expectation was *not* that which Jesus himself had in mind when he tried to impress upon his contemporaries the urgency of the crisis in which they were living. It would be out of place to attempt to substantiate this in any detail here; and indeed I have already tried to do it elsewhere.[1] Let me simply say that I am convinced, with much more eminent New Testament scholars than myself,[2] that Jesus' words about watching, and the imminence of the crisis, and so on, were in the first instance addressed, not to the Church, to alert it to his own return at some future date, but to his Jewish contemporaries, and particularly his opponents, to rouse them to the fact that their day of destiny as the people of God was even now upon them. On their acceptance or rejection of him and his message depended whether the vineyard was to be taken from them or not. The last hour was for them about to strike, that day of visitation of which their prophets had spoken and for which precisely their watchmen were appointed.

We accept the fact that in the parable of the Wicked Husbandman the setting is the long history of God's people Israel, upon whom the decisive day of reckoning has now come. So, I believe, in the other parables, which likewise begin with the owner going away and entrusting his possessions to servants or tenants, the point is also that, after the period of delegated responsibility, the Lord himself has come to his own: the faithful servants are those who are ready to recognize and open to him, the unfaithful those who, like the watchmen and shepherds of the Old Testament, are simply concerned with maintaining their own position. The call to watch is the charge to discern the signs of the times, to know what hour it is, and to be ready to receive their Messiah. It is addressed to all to whom the demand of the gospel comes, then and now: it is not confined, as the Evangelists, under the influence of first century apocalyptic, sought to confine it, to a single 'second' event within that generation or any other. The challenge comes to all men everywhere, as it did to the Jews, to recognize

[1] In my book *Jesus and His Coming*.
[2] Cf., e.g., C. H. Dodd, **The** *Parables* **of** *the Kingdom*, and J. Jeremias, *The Parables of Jesus*.

and discern that when Jesus comes into their midst the ultimate choices of life and death are upon them, that the last judgement has begun. When the Son of man comes to this generation too, will he find faith, or will it also prove an adulterous and sinful generation? When the Son of man is revealed in the crises of this age, as he was in the collapse of Judaism and the capture of the City, will you, he says, be taken with the world or will you find deliverance like Noah and Lot? Where is your treasure? For at any point the thief may break through or death expose you, and you may be found unprepared.

All these images and countless others in the teaching of Jesus are for us made entirely remote if they are restricted to a single cataclysmic event of which we may think, 'This year, next year, sometime, (or, for all practical purposes) never'. For the early Christians, so to focus them was to give them urgency and proximity, just as for them the abiding truth and continuous experience of the Fall was pointed and made vivid as the bio-graphy of a single historical figure. For us, in each case, the effect is remoteness and unreality. Without therefore abandoning in the least degree our sure and certain hope of the consummation of all things in Christ, we should ask whether we exhaust or even begin to fulfil our responsibility as watchmen to the men of our generation by directing their eyes solely to the *Last* Day. Indeed, I believe a too exclusive concentration on the End may be one of the most subtle ways the devil has of distracting men from the very points and issues in which Christ comes in power and comes in judgement. The adventist goes around like Johnny Head-in-air gazing at the skies and missing the judgements of God that are abroad in the earth.

The first function of the watchman is to discern. Nothing is more exacting than this part of our work; for discernment means having first a concern, at least as wide as that of the Prophets. For the signs of the Lord's coming, the issues by which he judges us, are writ over the whole sweep of the situation in which we live. They are not always, nor would I say usually, written in the church papers; and sometimes they are written exceeding small, concealed like a man's hand in one of those children's pictures you have to turn every way up to interpret. Nothing is more fatally easy as we read the paper or hear a remark or make a choice than to miss the Christian issue involved, and for the porter not to discern the knock amid the clangour of the world or the busyness of the Church. We see only afterwards that *of course* there was there something vital at stake; *or we see it only when it is defined in ecclesiastical terms.*

Let me illustrate this last point since it is one of the most common forms of Christian myopia. Consider, for instance, the situation in the Union of South Africa. Notable individuals apart—and what honourable exceptions they were—the Church there was really stung into action, and not simply into words, by the threat of legislation which would prevent people of different colours worshipping together. This was the point at which ordinary Christian opinion was galvanized. It is conceivable, however, that *God* was equally concerned by the earlier legislation which stopped them getting married to each other, or forming trade unions, or being educated beyond a certain level. If the Church can hear the Lord's knock only when it comes on its own door, the world will be forgiven for thinking that it is more interested in the sanctity of its own institutions than in people. And men will rightly remember that Jesus was not.

What are we watching for? It is pious humbug to say that we are watching for the Second Coming, if when the Lord comes we are unable to recognize him. For the Lord comes, as the New Testament interpretation of the fall of Jerusalem makes clear, in what often seem purely secular and political issues, in those signs of the present time which Jesus said his contemporaries could not read. Being the Lord's watchmen in these issues can almost always be construed as the Church meddling or interfering—or even be discredited by our fellow Christians as not 'preaching the Gospel'. This is the wound in the house of our friends that hurts most. But if we are not prepared for this kind of thing, then like the Prophet we should flee and get away, and not be ordained as watchmen of the Lord. The call to the prophetic ministry, which is laid upon *every* minister of Christ, does not mean that we have constantly to think of ourselves as perched on a watchtower. For most of the time it will seem much more like the humble and uneventful job of the porter. But any preaching of the *Parousia* depends, in the first instance, upon whether we are prepared for the prophet's mantle. All the techniques of communication in the world will fail without the person, and consecration, of the preacher.

Nevertheless, we must pass now to the second question, of how we do communicate what is regarded by most people outside the Church as perhaps the greatest phantasmagoria in the whole collection of mumbo jumbo that goes under the name of Christian doctrine.

2

Imagine that you had to sit down and write a script for Independent Television on 'The Second Coming'. It raises the relevant questions in a very acute form. Where on earth—or off the earth—would you start? And, since half at least of such a programme must be visual, how would you *picture* the *Parousia* on a screen—even for ten minutes? And how would you begin to make the whole thing relevant to the man going to work on the bus with his *Daily Mirror* tomorrow morning? Where and how can it possibly be made to impinge upon his life and experience?

These were the sort of questions that passed through my mind when, a year ago, as my début in this medium, I was actually asked to do precisely this. I have a shrewd suspicion that they might leave most of you as blank as they left me.

But let us begin where people are. For I believe there are two ways in which people do picture the Second Coming, if they ever think of it at all. And these can at least get us started.

The first way is by asking some such questions as these. Suppose Jesus were to return to this earth. What would he make of our world? Should we recognize him, should we treat him differently? And what would he make of us? Suppose he came into our home. Should we really want him around, seeing everything that goes on?

That is how people sometimes think of Christ coming back—walking into the middle of our everyday lives. But more often it conjures up an entirely different picture. Suddenly, in the twinkling of an eye, we shall be conscious of something upon us. In a moment everything will begin to dissolve around us, there will be a blinding flash which will transfix men in terror, and as they look up they will see, not the H-bomb cloud, but Christ descending in a blaze of glory.

> Lo! he comes with clouds descending . . .
> Thousand thousand saints attending
> Swell the triumph of his train!

That is the picture of the Second Coming that has really burnt itself in upon us. And as poetry and art it retains its majesty. But try to bring it down to earth, to the science of the twentieth century, or the next job in a crowded diary, and it seems utterly remote and fantastic. Of course, there are those who take it quite literally and tell us that it might happen this evening, any day, this year, next year—and who can prove them wrong? But most of us will shrug our shoulders, and say, 'So what? It could just as well be never for any practical difference it makes. And what in any case do they expect us to *do* about it—keep our eyes skinned on the sky in case we miss it, or go round with sandwich-boards peddling doom?'

But the real mistake, of course, is to take what is meant to be a picture for literal fact. We can see the difference between these two in the first way of putting it. No one literally expects Jesus to knock on his door this evening. He is not really going to come back as a man among men, walking this earth as he did before. That, we recognize, is simply a dramatic way of putting it, to make us stop and think. And it does. Supposing, it says, our everyday lives were suddenly crossed by his, what should we make of him or he of us?

And so with the other picture of the sudden coming in a blaze of glory. It is also saying the same thing. Suppose the end of the world caught us all tomorrow afternoon? Suppose our lives were transfixed in a flash—just as the H-bomb might catch us—and in that moment we had to meet eternity? It too has the power to make us stop and think.

But it too is a picture, a dramatic way of putting it. By using this language the Bible is not describing in advance a literal event that one could pick up on radar or see on television—any more, again, than the fall of Adam was a single such event. The story of Adam and Eve (as most intelligent people now recognize) is not describing an incident that happened only once, a long time ago in the Middle East. It describes what is always happening with men and women—and always has happened, go back as far as you will. And the same applies to the picture language at the end of the Bible. By 'the coming of Christ' it is not thinking simply of a single event that might or might not occur in our generation—and which in that case could only affect the one generation in which it did occur. It is helping us to recognize and live with a reality that is meeting us all the time—that has been meeting us ever since Jesus first came into this world, and will go on doing so till Christ has come into everything and transformed it by his power and presence. Eventually the reality of that presence will confront us in a way that we have never seen it yet—and that is what the dazzling picture of his final coming is there to convey. But that is but one among many pictures. The Bible does not confine the idea of Christ's coming simply to the *end* of the world. In his teaching Jesus used many other quite different pictures, drawn from the midst of every-day life, which have no particular glamour or glory about them. At any time he might come into men's lives when they least expected it—like a burglar at the dead of night or the boss walking in when you thought he was the other side of the world.

Everywhere, at any moment, *Christ comes in.* That is what the doctrine of the Second Coming is concerned to assert. The trouble about the phrase 'the second coming' is that it suggests Christ is only coming again *once*, and that till then he is well away. But you will not in fact find that phrase in the Bible. It speaks simply of 'the coming' of Christ, and the word it uses means 'presence'. 'Always, at every turn', it says, ' "It's that Man again". There's simply no getting away from him. Go where you will, wait till doomsday, you'll still meet him and he'll meet you. You won't meet him in the high street, you won't meet him in the clouds, literally like that. But his life, his standards, his love will find you in the end. Never again will the world be able to get away from the Son of man. For at the end of every road, *he* is there, coming to meet us'.

But it is not only at the *end* of every road, so that we can put off reckoning with him, as we say, 'till kingdom come'. Wherever we are, he insists on coming in. May be it was in the man we travelled up with the other day in the train, as we turned away and buried ourselves in our paper. *Jesus* could have been meeting us in that man's loneliness. Perhaps it was in that coloured couple who came asking for accommodation. Was there no room for *him* in our home? But it is not only in our personal choices that Jesus confronts us, but, as we have seen, in everything that comes to us out of the headlines—and in the more obscure issues that don't hit the headlines. In everything, Christ comes in. The New Testament writers could not describe even the most secular events without seeing *Christ* meeting and judging men in them.[1]

We cannot help using the word 'judgement' when we speak of the coming of Christ. For the world is not at ease when he is present—and that is hardly surprising after what it has done to him. No wonder the Bible pictures men as trying to hide their faces from him.

But it shows us another side as well. There is one place—in the fellowship of the Church—where it pictures men actually inviting him to come. 'Our Lord, come!' (I Cor. 16.22); 'Come, Lord Jesus!' (Rev. 22.20). 'Come and stand in the midst of thy disciples and make thyself known in the breaking of the bread.' Such was the call of the early Christians. For them too he was not simply someone who was to come again at the *end* of time. He was someone who kept on coming in, someone they knew and met as he stood among them in their worship week by week. 'Behold, I stand at the door and knock; if any one hears my voice and opens the door, I will come in to him and eat with him, and

---

[1] That is why the Apocalypse and the Gospel apocalypses, for all their danger if taken *au pied de la lettre*, are so profoundly important a part of the New Testament. For, unlike the rest of it, which is primarily concerned with sacred or salvation history, they are giving us a Christian theology of secular history.

he with me' (Rev. 3.20). 'It is the Lord!' (John 21.7). To the disciples their returning Lord was a figure of *joy*. And ever since Christians have been eager to meet with him, to welcome him to their midst, to know his presence among them.

Suppose he came back. Christians have no need to suppose. They know he comes back—and pre-eminently as he meets with them at his own board. For this is the point above all where Christ promised his returning presence to his friends. It is as though he said, 'You *may* meet me anywhere; but here you will meet me and I shall meet you'.

But this particular meeting-point is but to *prepare* us to meet him at all points. Shall we know him when he comes? Shall we recognize his knock? That depends very largely on whether we have already got to know him and made him welcome in our lives. Shall we be able to see the moral issue in tomorrow's headlines, shall we be able next time to see the *person* behind the coloured skin? And if we do, can we face it, can we face *him*? That depends on whether we are used to looking for Christ, on whether we expect him to be there and count on him coming in. And all these choices build up, and make us by the way we choose the sort of people we shall be when *finally* we have to face him—that Man whom we have either learnt to live with and to love, or from whom we have turned away, on this occasion, or this, or that.

It is right that we should close upon the Last Day, upon the consummation of Christ's work—for that indeed is what the *Parousia* myth is about. All I am pleading for is that in our preaching of it we do not forget the other New Testament truth, that we are even now living in 'the last hour' (I John 2.18). 'The End' for the Christian is not, as for the Jew, the description simply of what is to take place *after* everything else. It is the description of what has already been inaugurated in Christ. The beginning of the End is the moment at which Jesus uttered a loud cry and said, 'It is finished!' The myth of the End concerns what is true, is being made true, and has still to be made true, from the Passion onwards. 'From now on', said Jesus at his trial, 'you will see the Son of man seated at the right hand of Power, and coming on the clouds of heaven' (Matt. 26.64). The *Parousia* is Christ coming to his own, in every sense of that phrase—and *through his own* coming into the whole of life, and claiming this world till all of it is his.

'We give thanks to thee, Lord God almighty, who art and who wast, that thou hast taken thy great power and begun to reign' (Rev. 11.17): 'Even so. Come, Lord Jesus!' (Rev. 22.20). It is by holding these two statements together that the proportion of the New Testament faith and hope is preserved. The expectation of Christ, in the double sense of that phrase, is not merely 'waiting for God's Son from heaven' (I Thess. 1.10), but the Son himself 'waiting until his enemies shall be made a stool for his feet' (Heb. 10.13). The *Parousia* is Christ coming into everything until he is all in all. And that part of Christian doctrine whose specific purpose is to insist that Christ comes into everything should not surely be the most difficult to make relevant.